Fron Tynemouth to the Tweed

*From
Tynemouth
to
the Tweed*

H.G.Dobson

© Harry Dobson 2005

All rights reserved. No part of this publication may be reproduced or transmitted in any form or by any means, electronic or mechanical, including photocopying, recording or by any information storage and retrieval system, without prior permission, in writing, from Harry Dobson, "Westaways", 1 High Stobhill, Morpeth, Northumberland NE61 2TT (01670 510694).

ISBN 0-9531840-6-4

Published by H G Dobson

Printed and bound by Martins the Printers Ltd, Sea View Works, Spittal, Berwick upon Tweed.

Cover photographs:

Cannon from Admiral Collingwood's ship, the Royal Sovereign, overlooking the river at Tynemouth.

View south, across the River Tweed into Scotland, from the garden of Cornhill House.

Contents

Tynemouth	The Castle; The Priory; The Percy Chapel; The Brigade Watch House, The Collingwood Monument, The Old Railway Station
Cullercoats	St George's Church; The Watch Club House; The Lifeboat Station; The Fairies' Caves; The Bay; The North Pier, The Dove Marine Laboratory
Whitley Bay	The Spanish City; St Mary's Island
Seaton Sluice	The Harbour; The Watch House; The King's Arms; The Octagon
Seaton Delaval	The Hall
Cramlington	St Nicholas' Church; Arcot Hall (Dudley)
Hartford	The Hall
Bedlington	St Cuthbert's Church; The Bedlington Terrier; The Market Cross; The Sun Inn; The Grapes Inn; The Primitive Methodist Church; The Trotter Memorial
Morpeth	Wansbeck House; Dr Robert Morrison and Bullersgreen; The Beeswing; Bow Villa
Longhorsley	Horsley Tower; Linden Hall
Weldon Bridge	The Bridge; The Anglers' Arms; The Priory (Brinkburn)
Longframlington	Embleton Hall (Hotel)
Lemmington	The Hall
Whittingham	The Tower; St Bartholomew's Church
(West) Bolton	The Hall
Roddam	The Hall
Shawdon	The Hall
Ilderton	The Glebe
Lilburn	The Tower
Wooler	Josephine Butler; "Fallowfield", Queen's Road
Yeavering (Ad-Gefrin)	The Monument
Kirknewton	St Gregory's Church
Ford	The Castle; St Michael's Church; The Village
Heatherslaw	The Mill; The Light Railway
Etal	The Village
Branxton	Flodden Field; St Paul's Church
Cornhill	The Collingwood Arms Hotel; Cornhill House

Index of Plates

1.	Tynemouth	The Long Sands
2.	Cullercoats	The Lifeboat Station
3.	Seaton Sluice	The Octagon
4.	St Mary's Island	The Lighthouse
5.	Seaton Delaval	The Hall
6.	Hartford	The Hall
7.	Bedlington	The Bedlington Terrier
8.	Longhorsley	Horsley Tower
9.	Brinkburn	The Priory Church of St Peter and St Paul
10.	Lemmington	The Hall
11.	Whittingham	St Bartholomew's Church (Chancel Window)
12.	Lilburn	The Tower
13.	Akeld (near Wooler)	The River Glen and Yeavering Bell
14.	Kirknewton	The Church of St Gregory the Great
15.	Etal	The Light Railway
16.	Branxton	The Flodden Monument

Foreword

"From Tynemouth to the Tweed" is the third book in a trilogy illustrating my 'photographic odyssey' up and down Northumberland.

That I have taken certain liberties in the planning of my route cannot be denied for, having journeyed up the coast only as far as Seaton Sluice, I then made my way inland to Seaton Delaval, north-west to Cramlington, Bedlington and Morpeth before, eventually, joining the A697, some two miles north of that town. Thereafter, I followed the thread of this arterial highway – with a number of diversions along the way – until, finally, I arrived in Cornhill-on-Tweed.

Having previously travelled the Coastal Route, from Blyth to Berwick and back, via the A1 Trunk Road, to Morpeth, the purpose of this particular volume is exactly the same as the two earlier publications – simply to acquaint the reader, by means of photographic evidence, with some of the many captivating and historically fascinating 'wonders' skirting this route to Scotland.

Of course I allowed myself a generous licence: how else could I have included such extraordinary venues as Seaton Delaval Hall, Brinkburn Priory, the Towers at Whittingham and Lilburn, Kirknewton's lovely church, the Castle and village at Ford or the battlefield at Flodden?

If other subjects are conspicuous by their absence it is likely they have already appeared in other of my books but, by omitting some I have thus been able to include others – a price I consider worth paying.

You are never far from history in our beloved 'hidden Kingdom': everywhere you turn you are confronted by reminders of our rich heritage – a belief I hope to share with my readers as they study the contents of "From Tynemouth to the Tweed".

Acknowledgements

Tynemouth Castle, Priory and Chapel (English Heritage); Seaton Delaval Hall (Lord Hastings); Arcot Hall (The Committee and Secretary of the Golf Club); Hartford Hall (Hartford Estates Limited); Bow Villa (Mr and Mrs G Teasdale); Horsley Tower (Mr and Mrs I Elliott); Linden Hall (Mr Bernard Bloodworth, Director); Brinkburn Priory (English Heritage); Embleton Hall (Mr Trevor Thorne); Lemmington Hall (Sir Charles Aitchison, Bart); Whittingham Tower (Lord Ravensworth and the Hon. T A H Liddell); Bolton Hall (Mr and Mrs J H Young); Roddam Hall (Lord Vinson); Shawdon Hall (Major R F H Cowen); Ilderton Glebe (Mr and Mrs T W Sale); Lilburn Tower (Mr and Mrs Duncan Davidson); Ford Castle and Heatherslaw Mill (Lord Joicey and Ford & Etal Estates) and Cornhill House (Mr Eric Grounds).

In addition, I am grateful for the continuing support of my wife, Susan, and for the time and invaluable assistance of both Ron Hodgson and Pat Hughes.

The Castle   (Tynemouth)

The history of Tynemouth Castle is closely bound up with that of the Priory. A site so naturally strong and commanding has always attracted the military minded.

It is likely that the Romans built a fort here. Since Saxon times a church and fortification have stood on the site. The Norman, Robert de Mowbray, unsuccessfully defied his king (William Rufus), here and remains of a Norman motte and bailey castle lie under the Elizabeth earthworks, to the south of the gate-house.

The castle stands on a rocky headland with the sea on three sides: north, east and south. The west is defended by the castle proper, which has many Elizabeth military works in front of it.

Licence to crenellate was granted in 1296 and it was then that the headland was encircled with walls and towers.

Like Bothal and Dunstanburgh, Tynemouth Castle is of the 'Gate-House' type …the Gate-House also serving as a Keep. Defending it is a Barbican, similar to that at Alnwick and quite possibly copied from it.

To the south the remains of a gallery and a solid, 13th century tower, still stand but most of the South Wall was destroyed in 1851. Much of the North and East Walls have also fallen into the sea.

The Castle   (Tynemouth)

The Barbican.

The Castle (Tynemouth)

The Gateway and Barbican – from the south-west.

The Priory of St Mary and St Oswin   (Tynemouth)

The history of Tynemouth Priory and a description of the ancient structure is already comprehensively documented and it is not my intention to repeat it here: a brief summary of some parts of it will more than suffice.

For well over thirteen hundred years monastic buildings of one sort or another have occupied this site.

Edwin, the first Christian King of Northumbria, built a wooden chapel here shortly after 627. This simple structure was replaced c640 by a stone edifice, built by his successor, Oswald, who had for a number of years in his early life lived in exile on the tiny Scottish island of Iona where he had received his Christian faith from the Irish monks who lived and worked there.

The priory has had a chequered history. It was first plundered and burned by the Danes, in 865, when the nuns of St Hilda having fled from Hartlepool to seek refuge at Tynemouth were then mercilessly martyred. In 870 it was again the scene of utter devastation.

In the reign of Edward the Confessor it became the fortress of Earl Tostig, brother of the Saxon King, Harold (he who was killed at the Battle of Hastings, in October 1066). Since earliest times this headland has been fortified: priory and castle are practically inseparable.

Before Tostig could re-found the monastery he too was killed, in the same year as his brother, at the Battle of Stamford Bridge.

In 1075, 'deserted and roofless', it was given to the monks of Jarrow by Waltheof, the Earl of Northumberland.

The priory was rebuilt, however, c1100 and it became virtually a place of exile for monks, from other monasteries, whose abbots found them to be of a difficult or wayward disposition.

In the middle of the 16th century a royal garrison was billeted here though the nave of the church continued to be used by the good souls of Tynemouth until 1668.

The Priory of St Mary and St Oswin   (Tynemouth)

The present ruins are really quite substantial.
The gateway, built c1400, is easily recognisable. Most of the curtain wall has gone but enough remains of the north and south walls to show where the vault began and the bases of the Norman pillars can still be seen.

The east wall (featured) rises to an extraordinary height with three tiers of lancet windows, soaring upwards – the centre window is nearly 20 feet high. The nave still has its west front, dating from c1220 and is entered by a doorway flanked by an arcade of blind arches. The monks' chancel is the finest feature of the priory's remains.

The Percy Chapel (or Chantry)   (Tynemouth Priory)

Attached to the east end of the priory chancel and measuring, internally, only some fifteen feet by twelve, is the small, vaulted, 15th century Percy Chapel – entered by a door beneath a stone figure of the Virgin Mary. The chapel has a vaulted roof with curiously intersecting ribs terminating in fifteen 'bosses' (ie 'studs' or raised ornaments), adorned with the figures of Christ, the Virgin Mary and the Twelve Apostles, surrounded by legends which are now nearly effaced.

Inside the chapel (which at one time was used by the Board of Ordnance as a powder magazine or munitions store) can be seen the arms of the Delavals and several heraldic bearings of the Percy family.

The chapel was carefully restored, in 1852, by Newcastle architect, John Dobson.

Photographed by kind permission of English Heritage.

The Brigade Watch Club House (Tynemouth)

The Tynemouth Life Brigade, formed on the 5th of December, 1869, was the very first Volunteer Life Brigade anywhere in the country.

In the Club House (built in 1886-7), which is now a museum, there is a searchlight and a wireless installation, a breeches-buoy, rocket lifelines and numerous model ships and ships' figureheads.

The statue of Admiral Lord Cuthbert Collingwood can be seen peeping above the roof of the Club House, left of centre.

The Collingwood Monument   (Tynemouth)

The monument stands on Galley Hill, overlooking the sea and the entrance to the river.

Erected in 1847 the fifty feet high pedestal was designed by John Dobson of Newcastle and the massive twenty-three feet statue is the creation of James Graham Lough.

The four cannon, flanking the steps of the pedestal, were placed there in 1848 and are from Collingwood's ship the Royal Sovereign, on which he served as second-in-command under Lord Nelson at the Battle of Trafalgar, in 1805.

Both Collingwood (a Northumbrian) and his illustrious commander are buried in St. Paul's Cathedral.

The hollow to the north of the monument is called the Howland and, in ancient times, it contained the Priory's fish-pond.

The Old Railway Station   (Oxford Street, Tynemouth)

The first Tynemouth Station was the property of the Newcastle and Berwick Railway Company.

Built in 1846-7, the station is Tudor-style and built of ashlar.

It has, says Pevsner, "an arched porch to give shelter and a coat-of-arms to add dignity."

The station was restored in 1986-7 and both the adjoining hotel and refreshment rooms, beside the platform, have now disappeared.

Cullercoats

Four hundred years ago Cullercoats did not exist. A few isolated farmsteads working the nearby land but the bay itself remained a peaceful haven. The village is said to derive its name from the Anglo-Saxon "Culfre Cotes", ie dovecotes, and to have had connections with Tynemouth Priory. The village stands on the edge of a cliff overlooking the picturesque little bay below, a mile or so from Tynemouth.

Three centuries ago coal mining and salt panning began in the area and the harbour was built to export these products.

A pier was built in 1677 but it closed in 1730: the present pier was built in 1848.

Cullercoats thrived for a while yet, sadly, within thirty years these industries were exhausted and the local economy collapsed. Eventually, Cullercoats made a spirited recovery to become one of the busiest and most important fishing ports on the Northumbrian coast. A hundred years ago the bay would be full of little 'cobles', their bonny red-brown sails straining in the breeze and waiting to land their catches of fresh herrin'.

The women of the village certainly contributed their share of effort to the industry. They baited the hooks and mended the nets and for many years were a familiar, welcome and colourful sight, in their distinctive blue jackets, long skirts, large aprons and black straw bonnets, on the streets of Tyneside where they regularly supplied city households with an assortment of cheap, wholesome, fresh fish.

Now, like in so many of our coastal villages, the fishing industry has virtually disappeared from Cullercoats – only a handful of boats leave the harbour to catch crabs, lobsters and salmon – when in season.

The striking figure of the fish-wife, with her brimming basket and her rasping cry of "Caller-Herrin'", is now only a near-forgotten character from the pages of Northumbrian history.

The Church of St George   (Cullercoats)

At the end of Beverley Terrace stands the large and beautiful Church of St George.

Built in 1882-4, in the Early English style, from money provided by the sixth Duke of Northumberland: it is a memorial to his father.

"Its tall and delicate spire," wrote one enthusiastic admirer, "so graceful in its symmetry, is one of the principal features of the coast".

Described a little less fervently, perhaps, as "noble, honest, earnest, yet a little cold," another critic does, at least, go on to say that the church "gives a fine accent to a drab sea-front".

The Watch Club House   (Cullercoats)

Above the north pier and on the edge of the harbour is the Life Brigade Look-out (or, Cullercoats Watch Club House, as it is sometimes called). Built between 1877-9 for Cullercoats Life Brigade as a lookout house it is constructed of rough sandstone with a hipped, plain-tile roof. It has a quaint little steeple, a wooden veranda, a tall clock turret and a shingled belfry. Below, on the foreshore, stands the Lifeboat House.

The Lifeboat Station   (Cullercoats)

Cullercoats Lifeboat Station was established by the RNLI in 1852. Before this time a representative of the Institution was at hand to recognise and reward any particular act of extreme bravery which is why, in 1827, a mariner received the Institution's silver medal: further silver medals were awarded in 1853 and, again, in 1898.

Cullercoats Station received its first motor driver lifeboat, the Richard Silver Oliver, in 1939. Tragically, that same year, six of the lifeboat's crew (including the coxswain) were drowned when a freak wave capsized the boat during an exercise off Sharpness Point.

In 1965 a C-class inshore lifeboat arrived at the station. This was replaced in 1991 by an Atlantic 21-class inshore craft – the lifeboat presently in use.

The Lifeboat Station   (Cullercoats)

The interior.

The Fairies' Caves   (Cullercoats)

Just to the south of the Dove Marine Laboratory (the site of the old salt water baths) can be seen a group of caves, once used by smugglers to hide illegal alcohol from the excise men.

The Bay   (Cullercoats)

The lovely bay with the south pier in the foreground and the north bay beyond – the piers were built in 1848.

The north pier   (Cullercoats)

The north pier at Cullercoats was designed by the celebrated Newcastle architect, John Dobson, in 1848.

The original drawings are presently housed in the Estates Office at Alnwick Castle.

The Dove Marine Laboratory   (Cullercoates)

Built in 1908 and sited on the spot where salt water baths formerly existed.

The building is now owned by the University of Newcastle upon Tyne and is used for research into marine biology.

St Mary's Island (Whitley Bay)

The one hundred and twenty-five feet high lighthouse, of 1897-98 (now an information centre), rises above a row of simple, stone cottages – which were built around 1800 – with pantile roofs and gabled dormer windows.

A little chantry, an offshoot of the old Priory in Tynemouth, once stood here, but nothing of it now remains. The only guide to its ancient whereabouts is a little inlet, in the rocks, known by the name of St Mary's Bay.

The Spanish City   (Whitley Bay)

A theatre and amusement arcade of 1908-10 built for Whitley Pleasure Gardens Ltd.

The high, stately dome – one of the earliest in Britain to be built of ferro-concrete – rises behind a three-bay entrance flanked by towers topped by lively bronze figures.

The Spanish City   (Whitley Bay)

As children, after the war years, a trip to Whitley Bay was considered a rare treat. When we thought of the busy, popular resort we immediately thought of the Spanish City: the two were inseparable – the Spanish City symbolised Whitley Bay. For more than half a century it attracted visitors and holidaymakers from all over the north of England and Scotland. Sadly, though almost inevitably, it has outlived its attraction and is presently (2002) being dismantled and will eventually be demolished.

The Spanish City   (Whitley Bay)

Bit by bit the various attractions are being dismantled and removed – the Roller Coaster, the Helter Skelter, the Waltzer and the Ghost Train as well as the many stalls and side-shows are now only a memory.

At the time of taking these pictures the 'City' has a strange and eerie emptiness yet one cannot help but remember, with vivid clarity, the smells, the noises and the pure excitement of a visit, as a child, to Whitley Bay's Spanish City. Now, one feels only a real sadness to witness the passing of this source of so much pleasure and happiness into the pages of social history.

Seaton Sluice

At the end of the eleventh century Seaton Sluice belonged to the Priory of Tynemouth. By the early twelfth century possession had been transferred to the barony of Delaval, where it has remained ever since.

Until 1660 Seaton Sluice was nothing more than a small, natural harbour known as Hartley Harbour and used for the export of coal and salt. In nearby Holywell Dene salt making flourished from the 13th to the 19th centuries with large salt pans dominating the local horizon.

The harbour was and always had been extremely prone to silting which, frankly, limited its usefulness. This constant problem was vigorously tackled by Sir Ralph Delaval in the early 1670s. He constructed a pier and arranged for seawater to be trapped behind a sluice at each high tide. At low tide the sluice was opened and thus the harbour was flushed, twice every day: hence the name of Seaton Sluice.

This 17th century harbour was substantially improved by Sir John Humphrey Delaval, who, in the 1760s, commissioned the blasting of a new entrance 'to better serve the needs of modern shipping'.

To this end he had to cut through a solid, freestone rock so that the sea could ebb and flow directly (east to west and not, as it had done formerly, around a bend to the north – *see photograph): both a safer and more congenial access and a small 'wet-dock' would be provided as a result. This new entrance (the 'Cut', as it became known) is fifty-two feet deep, thirty feet wide and nine hundred feet long.

At that time the seaward end of the Cut was closed by booms or baulks of timber (fairly rudimentary lock-gates) which slid into a groove – traces of which can still be seen. The landward 'sluice', incidentally, was situated near the present road bridge.

The timbers were lowered into position by one of several means: the certainty of which method was adopted seems to have been lost in the mists of time. Either a crane or a capstan seems to have been used but whether this was horse-powered or operated manually seems unclear.

This 'new' harbour was first opened to traffic on March 20th, 1763 and marked the beginning of a period of steady growth and prosperity for the village at a time when Seaton Sluice even exceeded the Port of Blyth in national importance.

Between 1750-1850 the village also boasted a large glassworks. In 1762 Thomas Delaval established the Royal Hartley Bottle Works (- away from Tyneside the only other glassworks in Northumberland was at Seaton Sluice) and by 1788, with three bottle houses in production it boasted the largest such works in the entire kingdom producing at its peak no fewer than one million, seven hundred and forty thousand bottles a year. The bottle works grew and grew, with its own 'city' of cone-shaped furnaces, cottages, work-offices and public houses: there were also copperas works, iron works, a lime-kiln, chapel, windmill, shops and market square – all in addition to the coal and salt exports. In 1766 a brickyard was established followed, not long after, by a brewery and then, in 1768, a shipyard. However, the village's prosperity was always tied to the fortunes of the port and, despite improvements, the harbour remained dependent upon the tides and weather conditions.

The Hester Pit disaster of January 16th, 1862 (probably known better as the Hartley disaster: a monument to the two hundred and four men and boys who perished as a result stands, sheltered in the graveyard of St Alban's Church in Earsdon) brought an end to coal shipments and when the bottle works closed in 1872 all kinds of shipments ceased.

Trade slowly drifted away from Seaton Sluice which was unable to compete with the improved facilities of its larger neighbours in Blyth and Newcastle. By the 1890s the harbour had been abandoned to the fate of the sea and its piers and jetties crumbled and were quickly washed away: the bustling, remarkable little village of Seaton Sluice which had for so long enjoyed unimagined good fortune had, finally, 'had its day in the sun'.

The Harbour   (Seaton Sluice)

The harbour, leading west to the present road-bridge where Sir John's landward sluice-gate was situated.

The Harbour   (Seaton Sluice)

This photograph shows how the original harbour curved around to the north, a factor which contributed to the problems of it constantly silting.

The Harbour   (Seaton Sluice)

The harbour entrance (from the north) previous to Sir John Humphrey Delaval's improvements.

The Harbour   (Seaton Sluice)

The 'Cut': fifty-two feet deep, thirty feet wide and nine hundred feet long – which was blasted through solid rock to make an entrance directly to the sea.

The Watch House   (Seaton Sluice)

Built in 1876 for the Seaton Sluice Voluntary Life Saving Company.

It has been said that it "looks like a miniature church, with a pyramid-roofed tower at one end".

The Harbour   (Seaton Sluice)

The tiny harbour was once so important it was defended by a battery, on the ballast-mount close by, and a party of soldiers.

The harbour entrance, or "Cut", is now bridged.

The building on the right is the Kings Arms.

The King's Arms   (Seaton Sluice)

An early 18th century building ' but very plain'.

The Octagon   (Seaton Sluice)

The rather quaint, embattled stone tower stands next to the roadway, with its arched windows and added right wing (which features a rather fine Venetian window), is called – because of its shape – the Octagon. Used for various purposes over the period of its three hundred years history – it is an early 18th century building – it has been the Harbour Master's office, a coal office and a newsroom: it was converted into a private residence in the 1980s.

Though known officially as 'the Octagon' it was for many years described locally as 'Katy's Castle'.

"Katy" was an old lady, Katherine Rawbone, who lived for some years, with her husband, in the old tower. The couple had no children of their own so, being the naturally kind-hearted character she was, Katy befriended the village children, to whom she showed many kindnesses.

It was the children who gave the tower the name "Katy's Castle".

Katherine was born and bred in Seaton Sluice and lived her entire life in the village, though in several different houses – including, for a time, the old Watch Tower (see photograph, page 38).

This popular and much loved lady died in her one hundred and first year.

The Octagon   (Seaton Sluice)

Formerly the Harbour-Master's office, now a private residence.

Seaton Delaval Hall

Numerous writers over the years have expressed their colourful and critical opinions of Sir John Vanburgh's impressive creation – some flattering, others not quite so.

"The most important 18th century country house in the north-east of England", is how one described it. He then qualified his remark by adding: "A superb but impractical house."

Another eulogises – "A grand piece of architectural theatre", and adds: "a masterpiece of architectural imagination".

One other, equally captivated, wrote: "This stately mansion; unsurpassed for grandeur and dignity by any other in the north of England."

Nikolaus Pevsner described it as "a sombre house of smoke-blackened stone, facing the bleak scene, with the smoke of Blyth and the sea in the distance to the north". In a more kindly vein, however, he continued: "No other Vanburgh house is so mature, so compact and so powerful… for though it belongs to the hand of its master, in every detail, it is yet completely individual with its own composition and mood."

Yet another admiring critic portrays the Hall as 'a lonely masterpiece acclaimed as unique among the works of Vanburgh and curiously sympathetic to the spirit of coastal Northumberland".

And what of the owner, the man for whom it was built: what did he think? Admiral George Delaval was of the opinion that the Hall "was universally recognised as one of Sir John Vanburgh's finest achievements… some people (he preens) consider it his masterpiece".

Seaton Delaval Hall was built between 1718-28 for Admiral George Delaval who had purchased the Seaton Delaval estate from Sir John Delaval, in 1717. Vanburgh was more than fifty years of age when he designed the house; the Admiral was older and both were dead before its completion.

The architectural details of the Hall are classical and the general plan, a square central block with arcaded wings running at right angles to it, is that of a Palladio villa, but the central block itself, "with its dramatically jagged silhouette and octagonal corner towers" has more in common with a medieval castle…

The centre block is one of the most uncompromising and original pieces of design of the period and the two long stable and domestic wings enclose a courtyard that suggests nothing as much as a 'stage set'. The Hall was 'seriously marred', one critic complained, in the latter part of the 18th century by the addition of a large wing extending the south elevation, seven bays to the east.

The Newcastle architect, John Dobson, proposed to rebuild the east wing 'to conform closely with Vanburgh's architectural detailing', with octagonal corner towers repeating, exactly, those on the central block. Dobson also proposed the building of a matching west wing which would have created an enormous south front of no fewer than twenty-three bays. The owner, at the time, Sir Jacob Henry Astley apparently found Mr Dobson's proposals 'unacceptable' and Sir Jacob's successor 'seemed little interested in building'.

In a letter I received from the late F Hetherington Esq (sub-agent of the Delaval Estate since 1946), in October, 1997, he wrote – "… there are no signs of John Dobson's work on exterior photographs.". "Dobson came here", he continues, "in *1818 and made plans for a grand restoration of the centre part of the Hall which were not acceptable to the then owner, Sir Jacob Astley".

Mr Hetherington is slightly in error here since Sir Jacob died on the 28th of April, 1817: Dobson must, therefore, have proposed his plan to Sir Jacob early in 1817 or possibly in 1816 but certainly not 1818. However, Mr Hetherington goes on: "The (second) fire occurred on the 22nd of January, 1822, following which John Dobson was commissioned to make the house both wind and water tight; the main works being new roofs with timbers on the east and west wings of the centre. He also strengthened the south with iron columns to replace the stone ones and by building brick arches."

(I am immensely grateful to Mr Hetherington (and his daughter) who, sadly, passed away in the year 2000, aged 90 years, both for his kind interest in supplying this information and through whose good offices I received Lord Hasting's permission to take my photographs of the Hall).

The west wing of the Hall was burned down on May 6th, 1752, but rebuilt to the original plan. The second fire, which originated in a chimney and is referred to by Mr Hetherington, reduced the main building to a splendid ruin. Only the sterling efforts of the staff, both estate and domestic workers, saved the two wings. "The heat was so intense", wrote W W Tomlinson, "that the glass in the windows was reduced to a liquid state and the lead on the roof poured down like water."

Seaton Delaval Hall has had a chequered, some would say unlucky, history. Twice badly affected by fire; left roofless for the best part of half a century: badly damaged by troops billeted here during the 1914-18 War, it was requisitioned again during the entire period of the Second World War (1939-45) when, again, it was treated with a great deal less than proper respect. Had the house, thereafter, been denied the necessary restoration it was in danger not only of becoming derelict but (the present owner is convinced) it was in imminent danger of total collapse.

As a result of the commendable efforts of Lord Hastings, after 1945 – including the re-roofing of both the east and west wings, repair of the stables, replacement of ceilings and the restoration of various rooms, simply to mention some of the essential work that was being done – the Hall was eventually opened to the public in 1950.

But, notwithstanding the marvellous efforts made since the last war to restore this fine building, Thomas Faulkner is of the opinion that it was the vital repairs, after the fire of 1822, by Newcastle architect John Dobson, 'that enabled what remains of the house's architectural glories to survive to the present day'.

Seaton Delaval Hall

The imposing north front 'with its dramatically jagged silhouette and octagonal corner towers' has more in common with a medieval castle… A flight of sixteen steps ascends to a lofty Doric portico whose superb columns, with their richly embellished entablatures, form a most commanding entrance. In the tympanum of the pediment above, the arms of the family and various trophies are carved.

The whole of the finely sculptured façade is crowned with a balustrade on which are arranged several elegant vases on pedestals.

Photographed by kind permission of Lord Hastings.

Seaton Delaval Hall

The magnificent south front with its portico of detached, elegantly fluted Ionic columns carrying a balustraded balcony and the wide staircase leading up to the portico.

Photographed by kind permission of Lord Hastings.

Seaton Delaval Hall

The square central block has arcaded wings running at right angles to it.

Photographed by kind permission of Lord Hastings.

Seaton Delaval Hall

The west front of the central block overlooking the gardens.

Photographed by kind permission of Lord Hastings.

Seaton Delaval Hall

The west wing contained the vast kitchen.

It was the west wing which was burned down on May 6th, 1752, but rebuilt to the original plan.

Photographed by kind permission of Lord Hastings.

Seaton Delaval Hall

The west wing with its Venetian window set in an ovoid bay.

Photographed by kind permission of Lord Hastings.

Seaton Delaval Hall

The gardens – on the west side of the house.

Photographed by kind permission of Lord Hastings.

Seaton Delaval Hall

To the east and west, at right-angles to the central building, are colonnades flanking the stables on one side and kitchen ranges on the other… this provides a courtyard.

Photographed by kind permission of Lord Hastings.

Seaton Delaval Hall

Two immense wings with beautiful arcades running along the whole length of their fronts enclose a spacious courtyard.

The east wing, containing the 'cathedral like' stables (featured) and the west wing (opposite) enclose a courtyard 'that suggests nothing as much as a stage-set'.

Photographed by kind permission of Lord Hastings.

The Church of St Nicholas   (Cramlington)

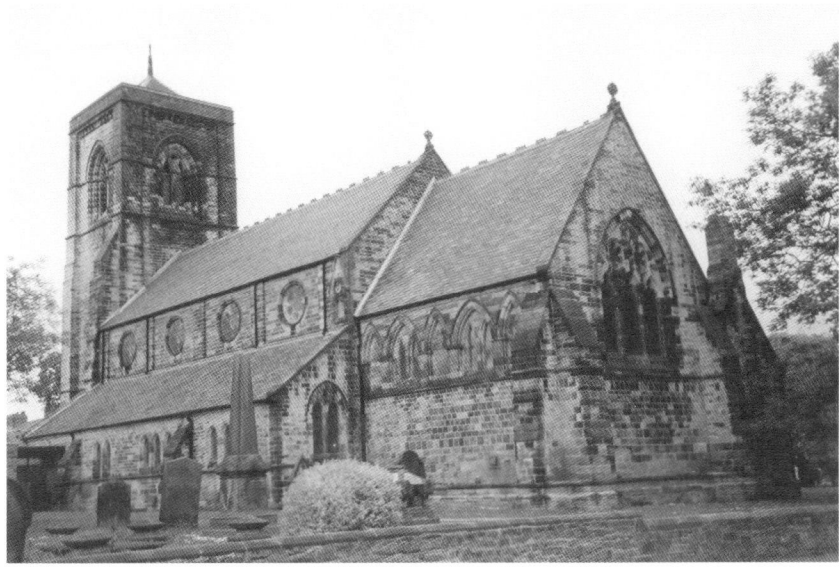

The first recorded reference to a church in Cramlington is the Chapel of St Mary, in 1135. In 1328 it became St Nicholas': by 1665 'it was in a ruinous state' and was rebuilt in 1680.

'When the extension to the present church was built on the site of the Norman Chapel a fragment of a Norman pillar was found.'

According to the Newcastle Daily Journal of January 16th, 1865, in the year 1856 John Dobson had proposed a Gothic design for the Church of St Nicholas, in Cramlington.

The Church of St Nicholas   (Cramlington)

Eva James, in her brief "A History of St Nicholas' Church, Cramlington", says that as a result of a faculty, granted in 1865, to build a new church, 'Mr Dobson of Newcastle was the architect appointed and three designs were presented: the one accepted was to cost £2,600'.

However, John Dobson died on the 8th of January 1865 and, moreover, had ceased to practise after his severe stroke in 1863 so while the designs may have come from his offices in Pilgrim Street (Newcastle) it seems most unlikely they were produced by 'the great man' himself.

Arcot Hall   (Dudley, Cramlington)

The Newcastle Daily Journal of January 16th, 1865, claims that 'in the 1820s' John Dobson made additions to the eighteenth century house at Arcot, which is now and has been for a number of years, a Golf Club.

It is an 'L-plan' house. Its centre bow (on the west front) is capped by a lead dome, similar to that on William Stokoe's Hartford Hall, near Bedlington, Northumberland. This part of the house (the bow) was added by Dobson for George Shum-Storey, an Indian adventurer who was present at the siege of Arcot, near Madras: it seems likely, therefore, that this inspired him to choose the name he did for his residence.

Arcot Hall   (Dudley, Cramlington)

The three-bay, three-storeyed south front has a most attractive Roman Doric porch, said to have been added in 1805.

Photographed by kind permission of the Committee and Secretary of Arcot Golf Club.

Hartford Hall (near Bedlington)

In 1832 Hodgson described it as "a jewel in the diadem of enchantment, glittering among the beautiful woods and grounds on the northern bank of the (River) Blyth".

Built in 1807 by the Newcastle architect William Stokoe (probably aided by his son John), for William Burdon. Scott's old print of 1811 shows the two-and-a-half storeyed south front with its fine central bow, flanked by symmetrical, single storey blocks. These 'wings' were demolished c1875 when the house was extensively altered. Only the central block with its lead dome (a Victorian feature) remained, though both a big porch and porte-cochere were then added.

Photograph reproduced by kind permission of Hartford Estates Ltd.

Hartford Hall   (near Bedlington)

The fine, wrought-iron gates, manufactured by the Coalbrookdale Company, at the north entrance to the grounds, are also Victorian and were proudly displayed at the Vienna Exhibition, in 1873.

Photographed by kind permission of Hartford Estates Ltd.

The Church of St Cuthbert   (Bedlington)

There has reportedly been a church on the site of the present building for more than a thousand years. The first known incumbent (a Saxon) was Eliaf Todd, in the year 900.

On Saturday, December 12th, 1069, monks, carrying the coffin containing St Cuthbert's bones and relics, from Lindisfarne to the safety of Durham, rested overnight in Bedlington. To commemorate this auspicious occasion a simple wooden chapel was erected on the saint's resting place which, later (c1089), was replaced by a stone, Norman structure.

For several centuries we know practically nothing of the history and development of the church in Bedlington. What is sure, however, is that the important expansion of the coal industry and the ironworks in the Bedlington area, in the nineteenth century, meant the church was no longer big enough to accommodate the increasing congregations: a much greater seating capacity was needed and so, in 1818, the church was enlarged. During these improvements three grave-covers and part of the shaft of a Saxon cross were discovered. These tombstones – now set up inside the church, beside the wall at the west end of the nave, close to the font – are carved with crosses and swords. We know that the chancel was rebuilt in 1736 and the blocked, round-arched windows date from about this period when, also around this time, 'the nave was turned through ninety degrees… and given a big bowed projection on the north'.

In 1847 the chancel was rebuilt again. Then, in 1868, the old Norman tower, 'which was genuine twelfth century', was replaced with the present Victorian structure and a new bell (still used) was installed: the semi-circular part of the nave was also constructed around this period. In 1911-12, the 1817 circular gallery was replaced by the Burdon Memorial Aisle. In 1921 a memorial chapel was created, from what had been a mid-14th century porch (later to become a vestry) in remembrance of those who were killed in the Great War (1914-18).

The south wall of the nave and the chancel arch, with its beautiful Norman ornaments are few of the remaining relics from the 11th century building – most of it now dates from the turn of the 20th century. A little window, by the pulpit, shows St Cuthbert clad in a golden gown, preaching beside a stream, to the shepherds and country folk of Northumbria – a reminder of the simple, saintly man who gave his name to Bedlington Parish Church.

The Church of St Cuthbert　　　　　　　　　　　　　　(Bedlington)

The south porch (of c1350) was converted, in 1921, to a memorial chapel and records the names of more than 400 local miners who gave their lives fighting for their country.

The Church of St Cuthbert   (Bedlington)

The nave is basically 12th century though it was restored in 1911-12 'to a more conventional form'.

The chancel was rebuilt in 1736, and the blocked, round-arched windows date from about this period. In 1847 the chancel was rebuilt again. In 1868 the old Norman tower was replaced with the present Victorian structure and a new bell was installed. The semi-circular part of the nave was also constructed around this period.

The Bedlington Terrier

When people think of the small town of Bedlington one of the first things likely to spring to mind is the Bedlington Terrier – the dog "with the look of a lamb and the heart of a lion: a warrior in sheep's clothing". He's been described as 'clever, tenacious and resolute; a keen hunter with staying power; a first class water dog; quiet except when aroused; nimble; quick witted; intelligent; charming; gentle and a terrific companion'.

The Bedlington Terrier hails from the small Northumbrian town with the same name and though at one time it was called the 'Rothbury Terrier' (doubtless because of its association with James Anderson) he was bred by miners who loved the breed for its gameness, speed, courage and intelligence.

The dog's background is, frankly, rather obscure. It is not an ancient breed though they can be traced back to the 1700s when, not in their present form admittedly, they were known as 'Gypsy Dogs' and were bred and used by Romanies. It is widely assumed that the Old English Terrier provided the basis of the breed with the possibility of crosses with either or both the Otterhound and the Dandie Dinmot terriers: the influence of possibly the Whippet and/or Greyhound has been seriously suggested in some quarters and strenuously dismissed in others.

The dog's origin is somewhat uncertain, it must be said, but one account relates as follows:

Early history credits a dog named 'Old Flint', owned by Squire Trevelyan, as a progenitor of the breed. Although this dog wasn't born until 1782 it is said that Bedlington Terriers, until the mid-1800s, could trace their ancestry back to 'Old Flint' through a dog called 'Scamp'.

However, the 'Bedlington' finally began his rise to a place of prominence among pure bred dogs c1820, for it was about then that a Mr Joseph Ainsley (or Aynsley), of Bedlington, bought from W C Cowan, a dog called 'Peachem', which he then bred to a bitch named 'Phoebe'. These two dogs produced a 'son', named 'Piper' – later owned by James Anderson, of Rothbury Forest.

The Bedlington Terrier

The dog with the look of a lamb and the heart of a lion…

Ainsley then purchased a bitch called 'Coates Phoebe' (the name Coates features later in the story), which he mated with 'Piper' and "it was from this mating came the beginning of the true-bred Bedlington Terrier".

It then took almost half a century before the 'Bedlington' was first entered into the exhibition ring – in Newcastle, in 1870, with an entry of no fewer than fifty-two 'Bedlingtons'.

In 1877 the National Bedlington Terrier Club (of England) was formed and by 1905 there were three Bedlington Terrier Clubs in England.

This 'official version' of the original and development of Bedlington's illustrious canine has not, it should be added, gone unchallenged.

The success of the breed has also been attributed to two brothers, Ned and John Coates, sons of the local vicar, for it was Ned who owned the bitch 'Phoebe' – the dog which was largely instrumental in 'starting the ball rolling', as it were.

Whatever the truth of it all one fact is beyond dispute: this delightful little creature is now one of the most popular show dogs in both Canada and the United States of America.

The Bedlington Terrier

The sign outside 'The Bedlington Terrier', a public house on Stead Lane, Bedlington.

The Market Cross   (Bedlington)

This stone, 18th century market cross stands at the bottom of Front Street. In the form of an obelisk it was nicknamed 'the Nail', probably because of its shape and the fact that on market days dealers 'paid on the nail'.

The Sun Inn   (Bedlington)

The Sun Inn had been completely rebuilt, though on the same site, before 1914.

In 1913 the owner, one John Irons, had installed John ('Jocker') Vickers Amos, aged 35 as his manager.

An account of the events which followed is well documented and easily available therefore I shall relate only the pertinent points of the story. On Tuesday the 15th of April, 1913, Irons accused his employee of being almost £46 short in the takings and having already decided to dismiss Amos he insisted he first of all made good the loss.

Amos vehemently denied the accusation and in the ensuing argument lost his head completely and reacted violently. During the course of the afternoon he shot and killed the wife of the fellow Irons had already engaged to replace Amos – a Mrs Grice.

Two local policemen were summoned to the inn to investigate the disturbance – Sergeant Andrew Barton and Constable George Mussell.

Amos, in his fit of uncontrolled rage, then took the lives of both police officers. Ironically, PC Mussell should never have been on duty: he was 'standing in' for a colleague. Sergeant Barton, who was already the recipient of several bravery awards, was fatally short twice in the stomach. Amos was eventually arrested, imprisoned, tried and convicted.

Yet, despite his heinous crime the perpetrator of these terrible acts received a great deal of public sympathy: indeed, almost sixty thousand people signed a petition in his support pleading with the authorities to spare him the death penalty – but to no avail.

John Amos paid the price for his terrible crime and was duly hanged, in Newcastle Gaol, on July 22nd, that same year, for the brutal murders he had committed.

The two policemen were later interred in Bedlington Cemetery.

The Sun Inn   (Bedlington)

The Inn, which was the scene of three brutal murders in April, 1913, overlooks the Market Place, at the bottom of Front Street on the south (right) side of the road.

The Grapes Inn   (Bedlington)

Halfway down Front Street on the north (left) side, stands a lovely, dignified, honey-coloured stone building now 'The Grapes' but formerly 'The Kings Arms'. Two-storeyed and of five bays; the classical front doorway has a segmental pediment and the windows all have keyed architraves. A bronze inscription below the ground-floor centre window tells us that 'in this house… Sir Daniel Gooch, the great… locomotive engineer spent his boyhood'.

Born in Bedlington on August 24th, 1816, he was scarcely more than a child when he acquired his first knowledge of engineering in Birkinshaw's Iron Works, where his father was book-keeper. The ironworks had first been established in 1736. The engineworks, established on the Blyth side of the river in 1837, was 'of international repute'. Over the eighteen years of the works' existence more than 400 engines were supplied to countries all over the world. Italy's first locomotive was built here, in Bedlington, in 1839 and is now to be seen in Rome's Railway Museum.

The Grapes Inn   (Bedlington)

Daniel Gooch left Bedlington at the age of fourteen when his father moved to Wales. In 1837 he was appointed Locomotive Superintendent of the Great Western Railway, by I K Brunel, at the age of only twenty-one.

He laid the Atlantic cables of 1865 and 1866 and the French Atlantic cable of 1869. He was knighted by Queen Victoria in 1867, the monarch insisting that no-one but Gooch should drive her locomotives.

Daniel Gooch died at Clewer Park in October 1889, at the age of seventy-three.

The bronze plaque was placed there by the Bedlington Society, in 1936

The Primitive Methodist Church   (Bedlington)

The church on Front Street West was built in 1893 for the sum of £1,500.

It is now a private residence.

The Trotter Memorial   (Bedlington)

The memorial was erected at the west end of Front Street, by the grateful citizens of the town, shortly after the doctor's death.

A keen social reformer James Trotter was also the political agent of Thomas Burt, who became the Liberal MP for Morpeth in 1875 and remained its representative until his resignation in 1913. Dr Trotter, despite living many years in Bedlington, was buried in his native Scotland.

The inscription reads:-

Erected by Public Subscription to the memory of Dr James Trotter, who died at Bedlington, July 8th, 1899.

Wansbeck House, Newgate Street   (Morpeth)

Wansbeck House is an 18th century stone house with a battlemented archway. It stands on the site of an old mansion called Bagpipe Hall, which was demolished c1750. In the early 1800s it was the residence of the Reverend Robert Trotter but by 1822 it was a private school. Later in the century Joseph Crawhall, the celebrated artist, angler and antiquarian lived here. His even more famous son, Joseph Crawhall Junior, was born here in 1861. There were, in fact, three Joseph Crawhalls – grandfather, son and grandson – which often leads to some confusion therefore, for the purpose of this article and in an effort to avoid this confusion, I shall refer to them as Joseph One, Two and Three.

Joseph One (1793-1853) came to Newcastle c1809/10 and at the age of about sixteen he began his working life as an apprentice rope-maker. He must have learned the trade well for in his later life he bought St Anne's Ropery, in Newcastle. He was an astute businessman 'with his finger in numerous pies', including shipping, coal, brewing and the arts. Indeed, by the age of only thirty-three he was reputed to be worth forty thousand pounds. In 1846 he was elected Sheriff: three years later he became Mayor of Newcastle.

Joseph Two, the eldest son of this "whimsical, rope-maker, artist and bon-vivant", was born in 1821 at West House, a part of Newcastle "with newer, comfortable, houses and gardens bordering on the Tyne". Joseph Two died in 1896.

Joseph One did not live in Morpeth but Joseph Two must have done if, as my colleague, the late A H Tweddle ('Town Trails for Morpethians') claims, Joseph Three was born in Wansbeck House, in 1861, and spent the first eight years of his life here before the family moved to Eldon Square, in Newcastle, in 1869.

"It is sad", writes Charles S Felver, "that old Joe Crawhall (Two) should be best known as the father of young Joseph Crawhall (Three), the able and superficial brushman whose sketches of birds and horses may be seen in many public galleries. Old Joe deserves to be better known: it was he, for example, who, in 1859, wrote 'The Compleatest Angling Books (that ever was writ, being done out of ye Hebrewe And other Tongues by a Person of Honour)" – and which A H Tweddle believes was published in Morpeth.

Joseph Three's gift for drawing was remarkable. His father had trained him to draw from memory and sketches from the period c mid-1870s show a sharpness of eye like his father's but a deftness of hand that far exceeded anything Joseph Two ever drew. He developed from a precocious child to a brilliant draughtsman and water colourist.

Joseph Two's sport was angling: his son's was horsemanship.

By 1880 his skill was sufficiently developed for Joseph Two to include much of his son's work in another of his books, "Border Notes and Mixty-Maxty" (published that same year). This was to mark Joseph Three's debut as an illustrator and there are a number of charming subjects throughout its pages done by him. The book especially demonstrates his capacity to draw horses, dogs and lively hunting scenes…. but his capacity for wit is also borne out by the amusing tailpiece of mice caught in a trap, marked 'The End'.

By 1880 Joseph Three had also begun to make a name for himself in some of the Newcastle Art Association exhibits but, by the end of the following year, he had begun to 'go his own way'.

Although he continued for a while to make contributions to some of his father's later books (including the 1881 reprint of "The Compleatest Angling Booke…." – which feature a number of amusing and skilfully executed drawings by young Joseph and his friend, James Guthrie) his interest in such work seems to have waned and he began to spend more and more time away from his family home (travelling as far afield as London, Paris and even Morocco) and the influence of his father.

Wansbeck House, Newgate Street   (Morpeth)

Wansbeck House (94 Newgate Street) was formerly the Morpeth Girls' Grammar School and before that the home of Joseph Crawhall Senior and the birthplace of his son, Joseph Junior.

It has two sections; that to the south (right) is a substantial neo-Tudor building and the three-storey brick section to the north (left), with rusticated quoins and moulded keystones above each of the twelve windows. The top storey is a later addition.

Wansbeck House, Newgate Street					(Morpeth)

The battlemented gateway with quatrefoil opening above the arch.

Wansbeck House, Newgate Street (Morpeth)

The rear (east front) of the house 'with additions'.

Dr Robert Morrison D.D., F.R.S. (1782 – 1834)

Above an archway, between numbers 17 and 18 Buller's Green, Morpeth, is a tablet inscribed "In Victoria's Jubilee Year (- 1887) this house replaced the one in which Robert Morrison D.D. was born".

There are those who would dispute this statement claiming that Morrison was born not in Morpeth but in the tiny village of Wingates, some nine miles north-west of the market town.

It would, I think, be prudent to examine the evidence before forming any opinion on this contentious issue.

Hodgson's "History of Morpeth" (1832), gives 'Bowle's Green' as the birthplace. The second edition of E Mackenzie's "View of the County of Northumberland" (1825), also gives Buller's Green and in his book the author states – "The writer speaks from a long acquaintance with this worthy and extraordinary character, to whose early acquirements he had the honour to contribute".

The following record, made by the Reverend Robert Green, Vicar of Longhorsley c1850, declares –

"Somewhere about the year 1770 a poor man residing in Wingates, of the name of Morrison, a clogger by trade and father of Dr Morrison the Chinese scholar and translator of the Bible into the Chinese Language, built, with the aid of some of the other tenants on the estate, a small cottage to serve the purpose of a schoolroom for the village and neighbourhood. Morrison subsequently removed to Morpeth where his celebrated son was born".

In an appendix to "Robert Morrison: A Master-Builder", by Marshall Broomhall (Student Christian Movement, 1924), R S Robson, of the Presbyterian Historical Society of England, supports the claim that Wingates, in the Parish of Longhorsley, was Morrison's birthplace. However, while significantly there is no entry in the Longhorsley Baptismal Register an entry can be found in the Register of St Mary's Parish Church, Morpeth: in a column headed 'Births of Dissenters' (listed under January, 1782) the entry – 'Robert, son of John Morrison, born'.

Robert's mother, Hannah Nicholson, was a native of Wingates. She married John Morrison in 1736 and there (Wingates) the rest of their family - of which Robert was the youngest – was born.

There is a local tradition that the Winter of 1781-2 was particularly severe and that while the rest of the Morrison family, including her husband, moved to Morpeth before Robert's birth (which occurred on the 5th of January, 1782) Hannah remained at Wingates to give birth to her son only moving later to join the rest of her family in Morpeth.

The 'evidence' to support this belief can be found –at the time of Morrison's death, in 1834 – in entries in the 'Tyne Mercury' newspaper, John Latimer's 'Local Records' (1857) and T Fordyce's 'Local Records' of 1867.

The balance of probability, it seems to me, weighs heavily in favour of Buller's Green being the likeliest place of Morrison's birth. Wingates appears to have little hard evidence to support its claim and relies heavily on 'tradition' – a tradition, moreover, which seriously suggests a husband would abandon his wife in the depths of an unusually harsh Winter, to a lonely childbirth, while he and the rest of his family fled to the relative safety and comfort of Morpeth – nine miles away. Surely in these circumstances, no husband worthy of the name would do such a thing. Why could James not have waited a few more days during which time he could –and should – have rendered such assistance as he could to his wife, then, after an appropriate period, he could have transported his entire family to their new living quarters. Oddly enough the traditionalists offer no reasonable explanation to justify this extraordinary behaviour.

I believe the argument in favour of Morpeth, based on the information available – especially the entry in St Mary's Parish Records – is overwhelming and that offered in favour of Wingates is tenuous, to say the least.

Readers, however, must draw their own conclusion and form their own opinions.

What is not in dispute is that around 1785 the Morrison family moved from Morpeth to Newcastle, where one of Robert's school fellows was George Stephenson – later to become the famous railway engineer.

Robert left school at the age of fourteen when, it is said, he helped his father make cobblers' lasts. At the age of sixteen he joined the Presbyterian Church in High Bridge, Newcastle, at which time he had made up his mind he wanted to be a missionary. Three years later he left home for London to study for the ministry. In 1803 he was admitted to the Independent College at Hoxton and one year later he was accepted by the London Missionary Society and sent to their college at Portsmouth.

In the fullness of time the College Principal told him he had been chosen to go to China. This was a particularly dangerous mission for the Chinese – isolated for centuries behind their Great Wall – hated all 'foreign devils'.

It was, indeed, a daunting assignment but one which Robert accepted with alacrity. There was much he had to do in preparation. He had to learn to write and speak Chinese since he knew that, at some stage, he would have to translate the Bible into that language.

Robert returned to London to study medicine for the ability to minister to the physical as well as the spiritual needs of those he sought to convert to Christianity would be an essential part of his work. A Chinese friend helped teach him the Chinese language as well as Chinese customs and together they often visited the British Museum where they studied ancient Chinese manuscripts. By 1807 Robert was finally ready for his 'great adventure'. Unfortunately, the political situation prevailing at that time meant it was not possible for him to sail directly from England to China: his route took him first of all to America then by means of a vessel registered in that country on to his ultimate destination, via the island of Macao, eventually arriving in Canton. Two years later he was appointed Secretary and Translator for the East India (Trading) Company – a British commercial institution. Hitherto and because of the hostility of the Chinese authorities his work had necessarily been of a covert nature for not only was his own life at risk, because of his proscribed activities, but so too the lives of any Chinese citizens who gave him shelter and support. But now that he was officially a representative of the East India Company he could mix freely with the Chinese merchants and the threat to his life was diminished – though he still had to exercise extreme caution for he was breaking Chinese law and the penalty for doing so was death.

He continued in the evenings to work feverishly translating the Bible and he was even able to establish a small clinic to help the sick, thus putting his medical training to good use. Emboldened by his small success and with the tacit approval of the authorities he also made plans to open a college for English and Chinese students, in Canton.

Then, in 1812, the Emperor issued a decree that anyone found printing Christian books in Chinese would be summarily executed.

Undeterred by this further threat to his life Morrison nevertheless continued with his work and in 1814 he succeeded in having two books printed – one of which was the New Testament.

In 1817 the degree of Doctor of Divinity was conferred upon him by Glasgow University.

By 1818 he had completed his translation of the Old Testament so that it was now possible for the Chinese people (or, at least, those who were able) to read the entire Bible in their own language. In 1821 he printed an English-Chinese dictionary… six books in all, covering some 4,600 pages.

Two years later he achieved the pinnacle of his success – his completed Chinese Bible was printed, filling twenty-one books.

After sixteen years Robert Morrison felt his mission was now complete and in 1824 he returned to England to discover he was something of a celebrity: he was even received at Court by King George IV. That same year he was elected a Fellow of the Royal Society. He quite properly presented a copy of his Bible to the London Missionary Society to whom he owed so much and who had been instrumental in sending him to China in the first place.

He remained in England only a short time. The lure of the Orient proved irresistible and in 1826 he returned to China where he spent the remainder of his life.

He died at Canton on August 1st, 1834, in his fifty-third year.

Buller's Green   (Morpeth)

The site of the house where Robert Morrison was born on January 5th, 1782.

The stone, immediately above the archway, reads as follows:

'In Victoria's Jubilee Year this house replaced the one in which Robert Morrison DD was born.'

Buller's Green (Morpeth)

The Bigg Market   (Newcastle upon Tyne)

Opposite Balmbra's, in the Bigg Market, the inscribed stone (above) can be found. The inscription reads…

Erected in 1897 by the Newcastle Bible Society, to Robert Morrison D.D. who lived in this Court from 1785-1803 and worked as a last-maker.

He went out in 1807 as the first Protestant missionary to China where he translated the Holy Scriptures into the Chinese language.

Born at Morpeth 5th January, 1782; died at Canton 1st August, 1834.
Morrison Court.

The Beeswing, 93 Newgate Street (Morpeth)

This Regency building, of c1820, is named after a famous Northumbrian horse that won fifty-one out of sixty-four races, between 1835 and 1842.

The mare had a distinct mark, like the wing of a bee, on her flank, and won twenty-four gold cups for her owner – William Ord, Member of Parliament for Morpeth, at Nunnykirk Hall.

This beautiful ashlar building has variously been a school, an off-licence, a general dealer's and an antique shop. In 1869 the licence of the 'Prince Albert' Inn was transferred back to the Beeswing – but it was revoked in 1871. It enjoyed "Beer House" status from 1878. In 1896 it became a photographic studio.

Bow Villa   (41 Buller's Green, Morpeth)

On the Morpeth map of 1826 the house is shown as "Buller's Cottages" (- there is to the south of the main house a small, two-roomed cottage). Bow Villa, a house described by Pevsner as 'a solid, square, ashlar house', was built in 1824 by Dr John Robb, who had come to the town some years earlier and married into the Nairn family … well-to-do millers!

He had obviously done well enough as a physician to be able to afford this handsome 'cottage'.

In 1856 the house had become the property of Edmund Bowman (b. 1808), an eminent railway engineer who had been educated at the town's Grammar School and who was for more than twenty-five years a Director of the North British Railway Company. Bowman lived in Bow Villa for thirty years, dying there in 1886.

At some time Joseph Crawhall the Elder (1793-1853), father of the famous Newcastle wood-engraver, Joseph Crawhall the Younger, or Joseph Crawhall II (1821-1896), as he is often referred to, lived here, though when, exactly, we aren't sure.

In Vivien Hamilton's book (1990, published by John Murray) "Joseph Crawhall (1861-1913), One of the Glasgow Boys," we read:

'The Crawhall family had previously resided at Bow Villa, Morpeth, but by the time of the 1861 census they occupied Wansbeck House, an 18th century stone mansion with a battlemented arch, built on the site of a previous mansion, Bagpipe Hall (demolished c1750). In 1870, after the family had returned to Newcastle (probably for business reasons) Wansbeck House became a day and boarding school for young ladies – later the Morpeth Girls' High School.

How long Dr Robb occupied Bow Villa isn't known. We know that Edmund Bowman bought the house in 1856 and as there appear to have been no other occupants save the three families mentioned the Crawhall's must have lived there prior to Bowman's purchase and after the good doctor terminated his residency – for whatever reason.

In 1896 the house was put up for sale – advertised as having the following: a drawing room, dining room, breakfast room and library, connecting to the conservatory: five bedrooms, bathroom and laundry: attic, two kitchens, two cellars, a pantry and 'outdoor office': also a two-roomed adjacent cottage: fruit and flower garden with *a fine spring of water and a tennis court – (*the water supply was at the top of Newgate Street and was considered a valuable asset).

The following year (1897) Bow Villa became the Morpeth Industrial House (and laundry), presided over by Lady Trevelyan, and the training of 'feeble minded girls', in laundry work, was undertaken.

Even as late as 1948 girls could be 'hired out' for simple household tasks.

In 1950 Bow Villa became a home for (though the term is no longer considered appropriate) Educationally Sub-Normal Girls, and was administered from Northgate Hospital.

The house remained the property of the Hospital until 1993 when it was purchased by the present owners, Mr and Mrs Gordon Teasdale.

The building has now been converted into flats though the east wing has been demolished, ' it being in a very poor state of repair'.

The cellars also have been converted, with windows that look out over the garden.

Bow Villa   (41 Buller's Green, Morpeth)

Described as a solid, square ashlar house of 1824 and often attributed to the Newcastle architect, John Dobson, though I have been unable to unearth any evidence to substantiate this belief.

Photographed by kind permission of Mr and Mrs Gordon Teasdale.

Bow Villa   (41 Buller's Green, Morpeth)

The small cottage adjoining Bow Villa, to the south, and built of three inch, handmade bricks, once contained a living room and washing and toilet facilities for the residents.

Photographed by kind permission of Mr and Mrs Gordon Teasdale.

Horsley Tower   (Longhorsley)

An early 16th century construction with a mid-17th century wing, restored c1926. The pele measures forty-two feet by thirty feet and is four storeys high. The windows are square-headed with hood moulds. The Tower has a barrel-vaulted basement, originally twenty-two feet by eighteen feet. The present entrance, made some three centuries ago when the gabled wing was added, is on the east side but the original door, on the south side, has been converted into a window.

At the east end are two smaller vaults, one of which leads into the 17th century wings the other may, at one time, have been a prison.

A stone newel (spiral) stair leads from the basement up to the battlements – which are in excellent condition. They are rather low and were probably designed more for decoration than usefulness.

A garde-robe (latrine) was on the second floor, at the north-west angle.

From the end of the 18th until the beginning of the 19th centuries the third floor of the Tower served as a Roman Catholic chapel.

When the nearby Church of St Thomas of Canterbury was built, in 1841, this function ceased. An adjacent enclosure, surrounded by a stone wall, was once a deer-park, and was also the property of the Tower.

There does not appear to be any record of when exactly the Tower was built. It is not mentioned in the Survey of 1415 and so it seems likely it was built after that time – by the Horsley family of Brinkburn. The ground floor room of the gabled wing (mentioned above) is known as 'The Lady's Room', perhaps after a dowager of the Horsley family or of the Carnabys, who followed them into possession of the Pele. The present owners are Mr and Mrs Ian Elliott.

Horsley Tower   (Longhorsley)

Built, it is generally believed, in the 16th century, it was owned by the Horsley family – from whom the village takes its name – it subsequently passed, by marriage, into the ancient family of Widdrington and later, in the same manner, to the Riddell family.

Linden Hall (Longhorsley)

Charles William Bigge asked his close friend, Sir Charles Monck, to prepare designs for a large mansion to be built within his estate (between Longhorsley and the River Coquet, on the east side of the Wooler road).

It is believed Monck prepared three different designs before Bigge made his decision.

Charles Lambert Monck (1779-1867) was born Charles Lambert Middleton but changed his name to Monck at the behest of his maternal grandfather, and, while supervising the building of Linden Hall, in 1812, he was elected to Parliament to represent Northumberland.

Monck was an ardent Greek Revivalist and Linden Hall (which Bigge named after the nearby Linden Burn) shows strong examples of this style in its four heavy, unfluted Doric columns of the portico, with its full entablature, frieze and cornice.

Monck supervised the construction of Linden Hall from the laying of its foundation stone, on July 30th, 1810, until its completion in 1812 and final occupation in 1813. Bigge's entry in his diary for June 8th, 1813, reads… "to Linden, where for the first time I slept in my own house".

It is thought Sir Charles enlisted the help of the young John Dobson to detail the portico and windows, after having returned from London, in 1811. Linden Hall was constructed in stone quarried from Horsley Common, south of Longhorsley, and Monck was credited with having employed some of the finest stonemasons in the country.

At the same time, Monck was also building the greatest example of Greek Revivalist architecture in Northumberland, Belsay Hall.

Begun in 1807 it took ten years to complete. This was his own house and, again, he is thought to have called upon the help of John Dobson to draw out and even cut the Doric columns of the portico and the Ionic columns of the Inner Hall.

Sir Charles Lambert Monck

Designed and supervised the building of Linden Hall (1810-12) and his own house, Belsay Hall (1807-17).

1. Tynemouth: The Long Sands stretch almost two miles along the bay.

2. Cullercoats: The Lifeboat Station and the Watch Club House (above, extreme right).

3. Seaton Sluice: The Octagon. The old tower was once affectionately known as "Katy's Castle" because of its association with an old lady called Katherine Rawbone.

4. Whitley Bay: St Mary's lighthouse is situated at the north end of the bay. It stands one hundred and twenty-five feet high and rises above a row of simple, stone cottages of c1800.

5. Seaton Delaval: The Hall has the plan of a Palladian Villa. The south front (above), with it portico of Ionic columns… approaches the gardens.

6. Hartford, near Bedlington: Built in 1807, by William Stokoe, for William Burdon; for many years the Hall was the property of the National Coal Board and was used as a Miners' Rehabilitation Centre.

7. The Internationally famous Bedlington Terrier: … "a warrior in sheep's clothing".

8. Longhorsley: Horsley Tower is a 16th century, four-storeyed, fortified Pele Tower, with a mid-17th century north wing – restored in 1930.

9. Brinkburn: The Priory (on the right of the picture) has been described as "the highest architectural achievement in Northumberland".

10. Lemmington Hall, near Alnwick: This lovely Georgian house, with its adjoining 14th century Pele Tower, was rebuilt and enlarged by Sir Stephen Aitchison, in 1913 "to its present state of splendour".

11. Whittingham: In the Church of St Bartholomew can be seen this decorative, chancel east window of 1880, with its beautiful stained-glass, featuring the figures of the four Apostles and their emblems beneath: (left to right) – St Matthew, as Man; St Mark, as Lion; the figure of Christ in the centre, with the figure of a sea-bird beneath his feet: then St Luke, as Ox, and, finally, St John as Eagle.

12. Lilburn Tower, near Alnwick: "Lilburn Tower is on a site of great natural beauty. It stands on a wide terrace with views across the Till and Lil Burns, on the east and south respectively. It has fine gardens and a magnificent approach road lined by trees for almost a mile".

13. Akeld, near Wooler: The River Glen with Yeavering Bell in the background.

14. Kirknewton: A place of Christian worship has stood on the site of the Church of St Gregory the Great since the 11th century – or even earlier.

The Bridge   (Weldon Bridge)

The stone bridge – made somewhat redundant except for traffic heading to Rothbury and west, up the Coquet Valley , now that a new road bridge crosses the river on the A697, from Morpeth to Wooler and beyond -was built c1760 to replace two earlier bridges swept away by floods in 1744 and 1752.

'It is well designed with circular openings in the spaces between the three elliptical arches.' The architect is unknown.

At the west end of the bridge is the five-bay, 18th century "Anglers' Arms".

The Anglers' Arms Inn   (Weldon Bridge)

This attractive, 'three storeyed', 'haunt of fishers and poet-fishermen' with its five bays and nineteen century, castellated wing, is an eighteenth century house, overlooking the River Coquet.

The Priory Church of St Peter and St Paul   (Brinkburn)

Brinkburn was already known by that name when, in the reign of Henry I, William de Bertram of Mitford selected it for the site of a Convent of Austen Canons, c1135.

With the consent of his wife and sons he commissioned Osbert Colutarius to begin building for Sir Ralph the Priest and his brethren.

The Bertrams made valuable grants of land to the priory but the 'Charlutary' (a register or record book kept in a monastery) shows they were often impoverished by Scottish raids.

A story has it that on one occasion the Scots had been unable to find the priory, hidden among the thick woodland, and so the marauders turned their horses northward finally giving up the attempt. The monks, grateful for their deliverance, rang the deep bells of the monastery in their relief. Alas, the sound of the bells guided the raiders back to their target only to leave behind them fire and slaughter in the peaceful Coquet valley.

The canons complained often and long (and with good reason) about their poverty – a Commissioners' Report of 1552 supported their complaint. In 1556, however, the Prior was found guilty of immoral conduct and his canons guilty of 'venerating a girdle of St Peter'.

The convent was dissolved and the Prior, one William Hogeson, was dismissed with an annual pension of eleven pounds.

After the Dissolution the priory passed into lay hands and a house was established on the site. The church remained in use but began to decay (in the seventeenth century the roof of the priory collapsed at the south-west angle) and regular services lapsed in 1683, although burials continued.

The Priory Church of St Peter and St Paul (Brinkburn)

The Priory is described as 'a large cruciform edifice, one hundred and thirty-one feet in length, having a nave of six bays, with a north aisle and transepts with aisles on the east. It has a chancel and a low, square central tower, upborne on lofty and well-proportioned arches'.

It is earlier than Hexham Abbey and it is possible its lancet windows have been copied in many churches in South Northumberland.

The Priory Church of St Peter and St Paul (Brinkburn)

The nave has three doorways, the most architecturally exciting is that on the north side. It has, according to one writer, 'an exuberant display of late Norman ornament'.

Above the beautiful arched doorway, in the gable, is a Gothic arcade of three trefoiled-pointed arches: bands of dogtooth run down the angles of the projection.

The Priory Church of St Peter and St Paul (Brinkburn)

The west end of the church is probably of about 1220. At the base is a blind arcade of six pointed arches. In the centre of the gable is a similar but much taller arcade with three very tall lancet windows. There are three stepped lancets in the gable at the top: all in all an impressive arrangement.

The Priory Church of St Peter and St Paul (Brinkburn)

The Priory House with its huge central bow and six Georgian-Gothic windows, inserted into the original east side of the house by Newcastle architect, John Dobson, who worked here at Brinkburn (on both the priory and the house) between 1830 and 1837.

The large central windows, with their interesting tracery, match those on either side of the bow in everything but size.

The Priory Church of St Peter and St Paul　　　　　　　　(Brinkburn)

The 'manor house' had been extended, in 1810-11, by Major Hodgson-Cadogan's father, 'in a plain Gothic style'.

John Dobson rebuilt ('remarkably successfully', so it was said) the older part of the house in a castellated-Gothic manner, a style he was to employ at both Beaufront Castle (near Hexham) and Holme Eden Abbey (Warwick Bridge, near Carlisle).

The Priory Church of St Peter and St Paul   (Brinkburn)

Drawings of Dobson's alterations and additions to the house can be seen in the Laing Gallery, Newcastle upon Tyne.

Photographed by kind permission of English Heritage.

Embleton Hall   (Longframlington)

It is recorded that, in 1675, the old hall belonged to one John Wardle. In 1730 it was conveyed to Thomas Embleton. In 1893, Dr J C Fenwick – whose family were landowners in Longframlington – enlarged the house, incorporating the 18th century west wing, with its five bays and pedimented doorway, into the Tudor-style Victorian building we see today.

The Hall is now a hotel.

The Victorian, main part of the building, with its fine pedimented porch, is on the right (of the photograph): the west wing – of c1730 – is on the left.

Photographed by kind permission of Mr Trevor Thorne.

Embleton Hall (Longframlington)

The two-storey, five-bay, west wing of c1730, now incorporated into the Tudor-style, Victorian building of 1893.

Photographed by kind permission of Mr Trevor Thorne.

Lemmington Hall (near Alnwick)

The history of Lemmington began some eight hundred years ago with one Siward de Lemmington, but it was probably a member of the Beadnell family who built the pele tower, sometime in the 14th century. The Beadnells occupied the pele during the next four centuries until it passed into the hands of the Claverings. Eventually, the tower passed into the possession of the redoubtable Fenwicks, through marriage, and it was during their occupancy that the splendid Georgian house, adjoining the Tower, was built, in 1746. The Hall remained the property of the Fenwicks until it was purchased by William Pawson, at the end of the nineteenth century. The south front has nine bays. The projecting centre bay has a beautiful Venetian doorway under a tripartite window and pediment.

The two ground-floor bay-windows, either side of the main entrance, are also pedimented. By the end of the 19th century this lovely, mid-18th century country house, altered towards the end of that century by William Newton, had become a roofless ruin.

Photographed by kind permission of Sir Charles Aitchison Bart.

Lemmington Hall (near Alnwick)

The pele tower is a typically 14th century, L-shaped construction. Measuring fifty-three feet by thirty-five feet, it is slightly greater in size than the equally imposing tower at Chipchase, which 'only' measures fifty-one and a half feet by thirty-four feet.

The walls of the pele tower are said to be some six and a half feet thick.

Photographed by kind permission of Sir Charles Aitchison Bart.

The Tower (Whittingham)

On the south side of the river, by the village green, in the village of Whittingham, stands what has been described as a 'Border Castlet'. It dates back at least six and a half centuries, for in 1317 we read that one Roger Purvays and the two others 'resisted the King' (Edward III) in the towers at Whittingham and Bolton. When Purvays was finally captured such was the strength of feeling against him that his captors petitioned the King that 'this open traitor and one of the greatest evildoers in the March' should be hanged and drawn. He very likely was. In 1416 the tower was owned by William Heron, who also held – among his several properties – Ford Castle. A century later, we read, the tower at Whittingham 'was suitable for a garrison of forty horsemen'.

Subsequently it passed to Robert Collingwood and it remained with this one family until it came into the possession of the Ravensworths of Eslington Hall – the present owners.

By the mid-19th century the ancient tower "which was formerly used by the villagers as a place of refuge in times of rapine and insecurity was repaired and otherwise embellished for the use and benefit of the deserving poor:" in short, "by the munificence and piety of Lady Ravensworth" it was restored in 1845 and it became an almshouse for four elderly couples connected with the Eslington Estate.

The basement consists of the usual stone, arched vault, with walls almost nine feet thick. An original doorway – a fine pointed arch – in the south wall and a window in the east show it to be an Edwardian structure of the fourteenth century.

The tower measures thirty-six feet by forty-five feet and is forty feet high. The present entrance was made in 1845.

A mural stairway formerly ascended from just within the outer door.

The present stairway is comparatively modern as are the corbelled battlements. At the south-west corner a square bartizan continues up as a turret.

After the Union of the Crowns (1603) the tower had its flat roof and crenellated parapet replaced by a twin roof with a pair of gables at each end.

These roofs were covered with red pantiles and were drained by projecting gargoyles. The roof remained thus until the alterations and restoration of 1845. Robert Hugill believes that the ancient pele, together with its out-buildings may well have been contained within a barmkin or bailey – a courtyard.

The Tower   (Whittingham)

Photographed by kind permission of Lord Ravensworth and the Hon T A H Liddell.

The Tower   (Whittingham)

Photographed by kind permission of Lord Ravensworth and the Hon T A H Liddell.

The Church of St Bartholomew (Whittingham)

The church is believed to have been founded around the time (737 AD) when Ceowulf, King of Northumbria, gave up his throne and entered the monastery on Lindisfarne, to be a monk.

The early Saxon church would consist, simply, of a tower, an aisle-less nave and a chancel.

The church would be as wide as the distance between the present north and south arcades and its height is reckoned to have been slightly greater than the eighteen feet archway at the west end of the nave.

(Facing the tower from the west, three feet or so from the tower to both right and left there are clearly to be seen two vertical lines of stones following exactly the same pattern as the quoins on the lower half of the tower. These two vertical lines are believed to make the western corners of the old Saxon church.)

Before 1840 the tower, with the exception of its battlements, was almost intact and exhibited the typical characteristics of Saxon work in these quoins and the rubble walling. The quoins, or corner stones, formed from local sandstone and still remarkably well-preserved, are arranged in a particularly unusual manner – a long vertical block of stone alternating with a short horizontal one, much wider and acting as a "bond stone" to bind the rubble walling of the tower to keep it together.

The quoins, it has been said, 'are the best in the county' and, indeed, are of a style not only rarely found in Northumberland but unusual anywhere in the north of England.

But, in 1839-40, it was decided to pull down this beautiful and rather unique edifice and rebuild it "bigger and better" in 'Gothic' – a commission entrusted to the Newcastle architect, John Green: a decision made, moreover, not by the worthy villagers of Whittingham but by their newly appointed vicar, the Reverend Goodenough.

W W Tomlinson ("Comprehensive Guide to Northumberland") describes the 'restoration' as "disastrous". Nikolaus Pevsner et al ("The Buildings of England: Northumberland", 1992 edition) calls Green's work "vandalism". In any event the destruction of the Saxon tower was mercifully not completed (the vertical lines of quoins on the south-west corner mark the point where the 'vandalism' stopped) and, thankfully, the lower half of the tower still remains and is linked to the west wall of the Saxon nave.

Inside the church the arch entrance into the tower, at the west end of the nave, is Saxon – similar to that in St Andrew's Church, Corbridge, built by St Wilfred and consecrated in 676 AD.

Its semi-circular arch and squared, heavy sides suggest a date of c900 AD. The way the stones in the walls are laid alternately, upright and flat, corroborate this date.

The Saxon archway was, for many years, blocked up enabling the tower to provide a safe refuge during the many Border conflicts. A strong door from the nave gave access to the tower. The archway remained blocked until 1909. Adjoining the Saxon work on the south side of the church is some 13th century walling, the lower courses of the aisle walls are medieval.

Over the past thousand years or more there have been numerous alterations and additions to this once simple church, resulting in the variety of architectural styles we see today.

The interior of the church is wholly in the Early English style. The Normans added a north aisle and arcade but, for reasons known only to himself, these were ruthlessly removed during Green's "alterations" of 1839-40. He replaced these ancient pillars and arches substituting imitation arches (- a copy of the 13th century arcade with its octagonal shaped pillars) in their stead.

The three-bay, south arcade and transept are genuinely late 13th century.

The south transept was heightened in the 14th century and re-windowed in 1840.

The south transept was formerly a chapel (or chantry) dedicated to St Peter, but all that remains now, below a trefoil-headed arch, in the south wall, is the old "piscina" – a basin for washing communion or mass vessels provided with a drain and set in or on the wall south of the altar.

In the 13th century the chancel was enlarged, thus extending the Norman structure.

Around 1725 another replaced the longer, medieval chancel. The remaining rounded uprights either side of the chancel arch are 12th century, but the actual arch, alas, has gone – a victim to the chancel's further extension and "Gothicising" by F R Wilson, in 1871.

The Church of St Bartholomew (Whittingham)

The church was dramatically altered by John Green in 1839-40.

The Church of St Bartholomew   (Whittingham)

The tower facing west.

The pattern of both the quoins and the stonework changes just below the top of the lancet window.

Either side of the tower, on the north and south gables, can also be seen the vertical line of quoins which marked the north-west and south-west corners of the original Saxon church.

The Church of St Bartholomew (Whittingham)

The unusual arrangement of the quoins (a long vertical block of stone alternating with a shorter horizontal one), here, in the south-west corner of the tower clearly illustrates the Saxon origins of the tower.

The Church of St Bartholomew (Whittingham)

The rounded uprights, either side of the chancel arch, are 12th century.

The upraised, pointed arch entrance and the decorative east window are the work of F R Wilson.

The Church of St Bartholomew (Whittingham)

St Bartholomew's small, 13th century window (with 19th century glass), is situated at the west end of the south aisle.

The original Norman, 13th century, north arcade was removed by Green during his "alterations" of 1839-40. Instead he substituted a copy of the south arcade, though what his motives were in committing this desecration are difficult both to understand and justify.

The Church of St Bartholomew   (Whittingham)

The three-bay, 13th century, south arcade with its octagonal shaped pillars.

Bolton Hall   (West Bolton, Alnwick)

A monastery once stood on the site of the south garden. This was 'dissolved' at the time of the Reformation. The site was then occupied, in the seventeenth century, by a domestic farmhouse.

In the eighteenth century it became a dower-house for Shawdon Hall.

At the beginning of the nineteenth century the celebrated Newcastle architect, John Dobson, added the plain, classical, south front.

Photographed by kind permission of Mr and Mrs J H Young.

Bolton Hall (West Bolton, Alnwick)

The east front of the Hall.

Photographed by kind permission of Mr and Mrs J H Young.

Roddam Hall (near Wooler)

At one time the Roddams were related by blood or through marriage to many of the principal families in the county. 'They were,' writes Leland, 'men of faire lands in Northumberland, about the Tylle river, ontyl one of them, having to wife one of the Umfraville daughters, killed a man of name and thereby lost the principal of 800 markes by yere; so that at this time Roddam (or otherwise Rudham) of Northumberlande is a man of many landes.'

The direct line of the Roddam family came to an end in 1803 when Admiral Robert Roddam died at the age of eighty-three. Thereafter the name was adopted by a kinsman – W Stanhope.

The medieval tower of the Roddams has long since completely disappeared. In 1973 the Hall was purchased by the present owner, Lord Vinson, from the last surviving member of the 'Roddam' family. Lord Vinson immediately embarked on an extensive programme of restoration and alteration: his architect was Thomas Bird M.C.

The north front (as the photographs show) was drastically altered after 1973. The top storey was completely removed: the vestibule, which had been added to the courtyard entrance in the middle of the nineteenth century, disappeared leaving only a small porch.

The Victorian windows were replaced, as they were on the south front, by those in the more attractive Georgian style; and the dark, courtyard surface gave way to a warm, far more appropriate colouring in keeping with the building's rich stonework.

As an almost inspired 'final touch' Lord Vinson planted a walnut tree which, thirty years on, is not only an aesthetically pleasing decoration but is now a mature and delightful centrepiece to an otherwise empty courtyard.

Roddam Hall   (near Wooler)

The old north front.

Reproduced from an old photograph by kind permission of Lord Vinson.

Roddam Hall (near Wooler)

The north front as it is now after the alterations of 1973-5.

Photographed by kind permission of Lord Vinson.

Roddam Hall (near Wooler)

The south front as it was before the alterations of 1973-5 with the extra half-storey and the old, Victorian windows.

Reproduced from an old photograph by kind permission of Lord Vinson.

Roddam Hall   (near Wooler)

The central, south-facing front of the house is early 18th century. Then, a rather plain block of two-and-a-half storeys with five bays and rusticated quoins, it was reduced by the present owner to its present two storeys. The doorway with its Tuscan columns, supporting a pediment, was retained but the windows with their moulded architraves, reverted back to their original Georgian style as part of a general regeneration scheme.

Photographed by kind permission of Lord Vinson.

Roddam Hall   (near Wooler)

Admiral Roddam added an east wing in 1765: the architect was Lancelot Coxon.

Photographed by kind permission of Lord Vinson.

Roddam Hall   (near Wooler)

The east wing… facing into the courtyard.

Roddam Hall   (near Wooler)

The west wing (featured) was added between 1770-82.

The wings, which contain much more detail than the central block, are each one-and-a-half storeys with five bays. Terraces, summerhouses and a mock, castellated, Gothic stable-block were also added: the architect, on this occasion, was Vincent Shepherd.

Photographed by kind permission of Lord Vinson.

Shawdon Hall   (Glanton, Alnwick)

According to Hodgson's 'History of Northumberland' there has been a house at Shawdon, on the site of the present building, since the 13th century when William of Glanton sold land at Shawdon to John de la Green. William's widow Joan, however retained possession of enough land for a dower house – and this, in 1296.

James Hargreave (solicitor) was High Sheriff in Northumberland in 1738. When he died he left the Hall to his sister Mary, who had married John Pawson. Pawson's grandson inherited the house and the estate, in 1817. The Pawsons were wealthy landowners, owning land in several parts of the county but, so it is said, they had a particular propensity for gambling.

They owned their own horses and kept greyhounds for hare coursing.

The story goes that if one of their horses lost a race which it had been confidently expected to win the unfortunate animal was returned to the stable-yard where it was instantly and summarily 'despatched'; the carcass dumped in a bog on the Shawdon estate. The same fate befell a dog whose performance failed to match its master's expectations.

Eventually and perhaps not surprisingly the Pawsons went bankrupt and the estate had to be sold – in part, perhaps, to pay off their gambling debts. The present house was built in 1779 for William Hargreave and the architect is thought to have been the Newcastle architect William Newton, though the style – both inside and out – is influenced by Robert Adam.

Additions and alterations to the house were carried out in 1825, by another Newcastle architect, John Dobson, and further alterations were made by Dobson, for John Pawson, in 1858.

Shawdon Hall   (Glanton, Alnwick)

The two-storeyed, seven-bay, south front has a three-bay centre with steps leading up to a lovely Venetian doorway. The decorated central pediment is supported by four giant pilasters and contains an 1817 woodcarving of the Pawson coat of arms.

Photographed by kind permission of Major R F H Cowen.

Shawdon Hall   (Glanton, Alnwick)

The four pilasters have characteristically Adamish capitals and the elegant doorway, with its flight of six stone steps leading up to the entrance, is like that at Backworth – "a Venetian opening in a recessed arch".

Photographed by kind permission of Major R F H Cowen.

Shawdon Hall (Glanton, Alnwick)

The west front has five bays with a central open pediment and a floating cornice over the first floor window beneath: there is another pediment over a wing set back to the left.

Photographed by kind permission of Major R F H Cowen.

Ilderton Glebe   (Ilderton, near Alnwick)

The tiny village of Ilderton is situated one mile west of the A697 trunk road, some three miles south of Wooler.

The Glebe, formerly the Vicarage, was built in 1841 by John and Benjamin Green, for the nearby 18th century Church of St Michael. The lower parts of the church's west tower are believed to be medieval (13th century) but, this apart, so it is said, "the church has little history because until the mid-18th century, when it was largely rebuilt, it and the parish were so frequently pillaged".

The vicarage remained the property of the Church Commissioners until 1937 when it was bought by Colonel George Craster, a brother of Sir John Craster – the owner of Craster Tower.

It was Colonel Craster who altered the east wing, in 1939, and it is this part of the house which now forms the drawing room on the ground floor and the master bedroom on the first floor.

The drawing room was originally two rooms; however, the Colonel's wife was a practising Buddhist who kept an effigy of the Buddha in one of the rooms which accounts, so I am told, for there being so many windows on the ground floor. Among his other undoubted achievements Colonel Craster was Commandant of the prisoner-of-war camp in nearby Wooler, during the second World War.

The various camp huts were situated on the site of what is now Glendale Middle School, in Brewery Lane.

None of the camp buildings remains now, of course (these having all been removed by the time the school was built in the early '50s), but, mounted on the gateposts to the western approach to the school are the figures of two lions – fashioned by Italian prisoners. There were also, at one time, other figures of ravens (wrongly believed by some to have been eagles) but, sadly, over the passage of time these have been lost.

During their enforced period of incarceration the German and Italian prisoners were obliged to work on nearby farms. None of them, according to one source, gave the least hint of trouble: the Germans, particularly, were only too grateful not to be on the Russian front.

They (both Germans and Italians) were occasionally permitted to attend local dances and the cinema and not surprisingly, therefore, there was inevitable fraternisation with the townsfolk of Wooler, so much so that, after the cessation of hostilities, a number of prisoners chose to remain, married local girls and settled in the area for the rest of their lives.

It was sometime during the period of conflict (probably around 1943) that Colonel Craster sold the house to the Reverend A Pawson.

This clerical gentleman only owned the house for some eighteen months during which tenure, unfortunately, he felled all the trees to the east side of the drive.

In 1946 the property was bought by Lt Colonel John W Sale, father of the present owner, who, with his family, moved into the vicarage in 1948.

Mr Tom Sale, in turn, purchased the house in 1974 at which time his mother, the Colonel's widow, moved into a bungalow at the end of the drive (prior to a later move to Lincolnshire to be with her daughter – at which time the bungalow was sold) that had been built by the Colonel, in 1951, for his gardener and cook.

Ilderton Glebe (Ilderton, near Alnwick)

This old photograph (date unknown and principally showing the sheep dipping at Ilderton), with the old Vicarage in the background, shows the building as it was – particularly the east wing – before Colonel Craster's alterations of 1937.

Reproduced by kind permission of Mr and Mrs T W Sale.

Ilderton Glebe (Ilderton, near Alnwick)

The south front.

The rainwater head, to the right of the conservatory, bears the date 1939 – the year Colonel Craster carried out the alterations to the east wing.

The east end of the south front now has a flat roof where previously it did not.

The ground floor, with its five windows, now forms the drawing room (originally two rooms) and the four-light window to the right of the downpipe is that of the master bedroom.

Reproduced by kind permission of Mr and Mrs T W Sale.

Lilburn Tower   (Alnwick)

The remains of the original tower of Lilburn are to be found only a short distance south-west of the present house: this was the seat of the Lilburn family during the twenty year reign of Edward II (1307-27).

The estate came into the hands of the Collingwood family in 1793 and the present house was designed, by Newcastle architect, John Dobson, and built, in 1828-9, for Henry J W Collingwood, to replace an earlier structure. Sadly, it was still unfinished when Henry died in 1840, whereupon the house and the estate became the property of his son, John.

In 1843 E J Collingwood recalled the architect, John Dobson, who was obliged to modify his design and make some quite serious alterations to the house, 'largely in the interests of improved comfort'.

Situated as it is 'on a site of great natural beauty' it overlooks the River Till and the Lil Burn, on the east and south respectively. It has fine gardens with balustraded terraces and a magnificent approach road lined by trees for almost a mile.

It has been described by one writer as 'a large, quite splendid house, in the Tudor style'; and by another as 'an elegant mansion … built from designs of John Dobson'. Mark Girouard (Country Life) insists the style is 'Gothic-Jacobean'.

When the foundation stone of Lilburn House was laid on January 3rd, 1829, there was buried in the foundations a manuscript commemorating not only the names of Thomas Wallace and Sons – the Newcastle joiners who, among other things, built the dining room furniture and bookcases from John Dobson's designs – and Ralph Dodds, a plasterer whom Dobson employed, but also Robert Wallace, Clerk of Works, and Robert Hall – the Alnwick stonemason whose exceptional skills were called upon by Dobson on more than one occasion.

Lilburn Tower   (Alnwick)

The west front.

Duncan Davidson purchased the house from the late Group Captain C J Collingwood in 1972. The Group Captain inherited the house on the death of his brother Sir Edward Foyle Collingwood who died, not only without issue but also intestate.

Lilburn Tower   (Alnwick)

Originally, the entrance front, like the south elevation, was perfectly symmetrical but, in 1843, E J Collingwood recalled the architect, John Dobson, and the magnificent porte-cochere – which, hitherto, had been situated in the centre of the entrance front, between the projecting wings – had to be moved slightly north (to the left as you face the entrance), 'to prevent draughts from outside finding their way into the main hall'.

At this same time the great staircase was separated off the hall.

Photographed by kind permission of Mr and Mrs Duncan Davidson.

Lilburn Tower (Alnwick)

The symmetrical south front with its towers and turrets and mullioned windows.

Photographed by kind permission of Mr and Mrs Duncan Davidson.

Lilburn Tower (Alnwick)

The east front.

Photographed by kind permission of Mr and Mrs Duncan Davidson.

Josephine Elizabeth Butler

> "The world as a whole is a better place because she lived:
> the seed that she has sown can never die."

Josephine Butler was born at Milfield, near Wooler, on April 13th, 1828, the fourth daughter of nine children in the family of John and Hannah Grey. Her father, John, was an educated man who was something of a reformer himself. He was extremely interested in the great public movements of the day and expressed wholehearted support for the Great Reform Bill, the Abolition of Slavery, and so on.

The first six years of Josephine's life were spent at Milfield then, in 1835, the family moved to Dilston, in Tynedale, and here Josephine grew up. She was taught to paint and become an accomplished musician: she was also very fond of animals.

She first met her future husband, George Butler, in 1850, when she was twenty-one. George was then a lecturer at Durham University. He was a gifted young man from a brilliant family – both his father and brother were Headmasters at Harrow School. He received his degree at Cambridge University then took up the position of Public Examiner at Oxford University.

George and Josephine were married on January 2nd, 1852, at St Andrew's Parish Church in Corbridge and the early years of their marriage were lived in the university city of Oxford. George later became Principal of Liverpool College and, finally, Canon of Winchester.

Josephine Butler became a social reformer largely as a result of the years she spent in the great seafaring city of Liverpool. A woman of great natural compassion and courage she needed to be so, for she took upon herself, and championed, a most unpopular cause – the condition of those women who had become, in the eyes of 'respectable society' 'social outcasts'.

These women were utterly and completely 'unacceptable' in a Victorian society which had different sets of rules for different people.

Josephine had been primarily interested in the education of women and had written a book on women's work and women's culture. Then, in 1857, the Butler family moved from Oxford to Cheltenham where the tragedy of her daughter's death occurred in August 1864.

The Church of St Andrew   (Corbridge)

Described as "The most important surviving Saxon monument in Northumberland, except for Hexham (St Wilfrid's Abbey) crypt", Josephine married George Butler here, on January 2nd, 1852.

Little Evangeline was only five when one day, in her childish excitement at seeing her father, who had just returned home, she fell over the bannister of the staircase. She fell headlong to the ground floor of the house and died almost immediately.

In January, 1866, the family moved from this place of unhappy memory to live in the city of Liverpool. As well as their only daughter George and Josephine had three sons yet, understandably, Josephine was overwhelmed with grief at the loss of her darling Evangeline. Then, one day, a friend pointed out to her that while the death of her child was without doubt a painful and personal tragedy there were thousands of women, in all the great cities of Britain, who had far greater sorrows to bear.

She visited the dock areas of Liverpool and was shocked and sickened by what she found there. The miserable plight of these unfortunate women was unimaginable. Her first action was to invite as many of them as she could into her own home believing, in true Christian charity, that no-one is beyond God's help and understanding. Then she established homes where they might be cared for.

Her actions and efforts brought her more abuse than friends. Indeed, when her name was spoken by 'society people' it was with contempt bordering almost on hatred. It was all very well for 'gentlemen' to be unfaithful to their wives and keep a mistress in the fashionable part of town but these wretches who frequented the ale-houses and alleyways of every port and city in the kingdom, who were violently abused by rough and common sailors and soldiers – they were thoroughly undeserving of any kind of sympathy and should be left to rot in their filthy, squalid circumstances.

Such were the ways of Victorian England. In matters concerning the law there was very definitely one law for 'gentlemen' and another, far more vigorously enforced, for women.

The laws regarding morality (ie spiritual behaviour) were grossly unfair to women and so far as women of the 'lower stations' of life were concerned these laws were enforced with callousness and often cruelty.

It was Josephine Butler's determination to have these cruel laws abolished that made her so unpopular in certain sections of society. But, subjected to public abuse and ridicule though she was, she remained steadfast in her resolve to have these degrading laws and practices removed from the statute.

Yet, despite this absolute and unswerving resolve, she was neither in her manner nor her views a 'militant' person. Far from it. She was a caring wife and mother who tried to persuade people to her way of thinking by reasoned argument and by the sincerity of her own example.

It has been suggested that had Josephine chosen a different cause to champion appreciation of her work and her memory would have ranked with the likes of Florence Nightingale and Elizabeth Fry.

The work these two ladies did (nursing and visiting prisons) was important and very necessary but Josephine Butler needed immeasurably greater courage to follow the path she had chosen. Because her work was considered 'unsavoury' it has never been accorded the recognition it so richly deserves.

In time, and as a direct result of her determined efforts, Parliament was forced to take notice of this able and dedicated woman who simply refused to take no for an answer.

Support for her cause at last began to grow. Many Quakers (The Society of Friends) were on her side. Florence Nightingale gave her support. Later many doctors and clergymen rallied to her cause.

She did not confine her activities to England, however, but carried her crusade to France and Switzerland; Italy, Belgium and Norway: indeed, she was one of the finest international reformers of her, or any other, time.

At last Parliament accepted the reforms she advocated and in 1886 the laws she so hated and had fought so long were at last repealed.

George Butler died in London, in 1890, and after his death Josephine became a prolific writer. She remained a widow for sixteen years and towards the end of her life she returned to her beloved Northumberland. For a time she lived with her son at Ewart, in Glendale, before moving to the house – 'Fallowfield', in Queens Road, Wooler – where she died on the 30th of December, 1906.

She is buried in the churchyard, immediately to the west of the tower, of St Gregory's Parish Church, Kirknewton.

Dilston Hall (near Corbridge)

Dilston Hall is a 'plain looking house' (much altered), built c1835 for John Grey, the famous agriculturalist and father of Josephine Butler. Josephine was born on the 13th of April, 1828, at Milfield, where she spent the first six years of her life. In 1865 the family moved to Dilston Hall, near Corbridge, which remained her home until, at the age of twenty-two, she married George Butler. The newly married couple then set up house in Oxford, which effectively severed her link with Dilston Hall.

Photographed by kind permission the Principal, Dilston College of Further Education.

Dilston Castle (near Corbridge)

In 1622, Sir Francis Radcliffe extended the old castle (first mentioned in 1464 and altered in 1566), when the tower was incorporated into a wing of Dilston Hall, and transformed it into a house. Nothing remains of this Elizabethan-Jacobean mansion which, in 1710, the third Earl of Derwentwater decided to replace with a new building – described as 'spacious, beauteous and commodious'.

In 1731 the Derwentwater estates passed into the possession of Greenwich Hospital. They showed little interest in the house and it quickly fell into disrepair. It was demolished c1768. Only yards to the south of the ruined tower the present Dilston Hall was built c1835.

Dilston Castle (near Corbridge)

East front.

In 1805 the commissioners of Greenwich Hospital had the castle's vault opened and they discovered the body and head of James Radcliffe the last Earl of Derwentwater and a grandson of Charles II, who gave his life in the Jacobite cause. He was beheaded on Tower Hill on the 24th of February, 1716.

"Fallowfield", Queen's Road. (Wooler)

"Fallowfield", the semi-detached, stone-built house in Queen's Road, Wooler, where Josephine Butler died on December 30th, 1906.

A plaque recording this fact, presented by Wooler Women's Institute, is situated above the front door: it was unveiled by her granddaughter.

"Fallowfield" is on the right.

Josephine Elizabeth Butler

Josephine is buried in the churchyard of St Gregory's, Kirknewton immediately west of the tower.

Josephine Butler's grave   (St Gregory's Church, Kirknewton)

"Every instinct of womanhood within me was in revolt against certain accepted theories of society and I suffered as only God and the faithful companion of my life could ever know."

Ad Gefrin   (Yeavering)

A mile or so east of Kirknewton on the road leading back to Akeld and Wooler stands this monument. The inscription reads as follows:

At this place was Gefrin, Royal Township of the seventh century Kings of Northumbria. Here the missionary Paulinus, in AD627, instructed the people in Christianity for thirty-six days and baptised them in the River Glen close by.

The Church of St Gregory the Great (Kirknewton)

In 601, Pope Gregory sent a Roman monk named Paulinus to assist Augustine's mission in Kent. In 625, King Edwin of Northumbria married the Princess Ethelburga, a daughter of the King of Kent, and she and Paulinus travelled north to live in the royal residence at Ad-Gefrin, less than a mile to the east of the present church. Edwin embraced the Christian faith in 627 and his fellow Northumbrians, eager to follow their sovereign's lead, were baptised in the nearby River Glen.

The first recorded incumbent of St Gregory's is one Stephen, who was priest here from 1153 until 1197. Very little remains of his ancient church and over the passing centuries the building has known a chequered history. Indeed, there were several periods when the church was a complete ruin. The last major restoration was carried out by John Dobson, in 1856, completed in 1860 – the tower was added some years later.

The Church of St Gregory the Great (Kirknewton)

On entering the churchyard one is confronted by the sight of twelve immaculately maintained graves. The style of the headstones is uniform and they are set out (as the photograph shows) in two parallel lines, seven stones to the rear and five to the front.

Twelve gallant young men are buried here, pilots who were killed in the Kirknewton area while serving in the air forces of Great Britain, Canada and New Zealand, during the Second World War.

They unselfishly gave their lives in the cause of freedom and for the last sixty years or so they have lain at peace in this quiet corner of Northumberland and in the shadow of the Cheviot Hills.

The Church of St Gregory the Great							(Kirknewton)

The twelve interred are:-

(Back row, left to right):

Sergeant J H Hobbs (RAF), aged twenty;
Warrant Officer G H Neate (RCAF), age unknown;
Flight Sergeant R D Maynard (RCAF) aged twenty-one;
Sergeant M A Dixon (RCAF), aged nineteen;
Sergeant R H M Macfadzean (RAF), aged twenty;
Flight Lieutenant M C Knight (*Flying Instructor) (RAF), aged twenty-two;
Sergeant G R Dawson (RAF), aged twenty four;

(Front row, left to right):

Flying Officer A B E Rutherford DFC (RAF) aged twenty-one;
*Lieutenant Commander D R B Cosh SSC RCNVR HMCS 'Niobe' – age unknown
Flight Sergeant C I Humphrey (RNZAF), aged twenty-one;
Warrant Officer II D M Flack (RAF), aged twenty-one;
Sergeant A V Jones (RAF), aged twenty-three.

The Church of St Gregory the Great   (Kirknewton)

There is a strange, stone relief, portraying the Adoration of the Magi, set in the wall to the north of the chancel arch, above the priest's stall. The relief is generally believed to be of 12th century origin but it has been suggested it might be earlier – perhaps 9th century. The workmanship is extremely crude.

"Kings in kilts" (St Gregory's Church, Kirknewton)

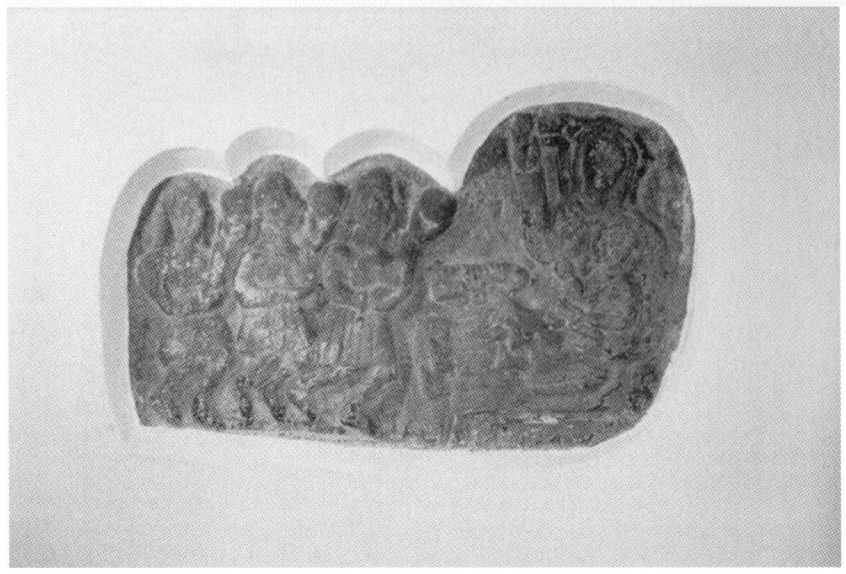

The Madonna and Child sit on a kind of trough while the Wise Men, clad in kilts, proffer their gifts. Behind the Madonna rises the tall figure of Joseph, his left arm protectively around Mary while his right arm is raised, pole-like, to greet their distinguished visitors.

The Castle   (Ford)

The castle is situated amid beautiful grounds on a considerable eminence (rising land) above the River Till, with a delightful prospect over the valley, as far south as Wooler and of the pine-clad heights of Flodden and the high green Cheviots beyond.

(W W Tomlinson)

The Castle (Ford)

There was a stronghold, probably no more than a fortified mansion-house, built on the site of the present castle, in the time of Edward I – around the year 1282. This was the property of Odinel de Forde, who died without a male heir and thus his estates passed, through the marriage of his daughter, to Sir William Heron – an influential nobleman who was Captain of the castles at Bamburgh, Pickering and Scarborough; Warden of the forests north of the Trent and High Sheriff of Northumberland for eleven successive years.

Sir William was a 'border baron' who, as much through circumstances as inclination, was obliged to take part in the regular 'skirmishes' which, at that time, were a normal feature of life on both sides of the border. As Ford is situated only some six miles or so from the frontier with Scotland Sir William was compelled to keep an ever watchful eye on his restless and predatory northern neighbour.

The old Hall he had inherited through his marriage to Odinel's daughter was incapable of resisting a determined, sustained attack and so, in 1338, he applied, successfully, to Edward III for licence to crenellate his mansion. William went further and converted his manor-house into an impressive "quadrangular, or courtyard, castle", with four angle-towers – the first of its type in either Northumberland or Durham and a model for others to later copy – "suitable to the dignity of its owner and sufficient to offer protection to the surrounding district".

Thus fortified, in 1340 Ford was raised to the status of castle for the defence of Glendale – an area overrun, as it so often was, by marauding Scots.

It was to be about half a century before the defensive capabilities of Heron's 'new' castle were to be put to the test. In 1385 a Scottish force under the leadership of the Earls of Fife, March and Douglas crossed the border and laid waste to the castles at Wark, Cornhill – and largely destroyed Ford.

The sixteenth century began relatively peacefully but it was not long before England and Scotland were again engaged in bitter conflict – this time on a far more serious scale than the regular border exchanges. On Monday the 22nd of August, 1513, and taking advantage of his brother-in-law (Henry VIII) being absent in France, James IV crossed the border near Coldstream at the head of an army of between 80 and 100,000 men.

Norham Castle offered pitiful resistance and lasted out only five days. Etal was destroyed and the inhabitants of Ford Castle knew it was only the matter of a short time before they, too, came under attack.

Sir William Heron being absent the castle's defences were left in the hands of his wife, Dame Elizabeth. She, perceiving this was a task beyond her capabilities, fled south to rendezvous with the advancing Earl of Surrey, Commander of the English army, hopeful of persuading the Earl to intercede on her behalf and beg King James to spare her castle. Surrey sent a message to the Scottish monarch offering two distinguished prisoners in exchange for the King's promise that he would spare the castle at Ford. Reassured by her belief in James' chivalrous disposition Dame Elizabeth returned home only to find King James had used her castle as his headquarters prior to his taking up his position at Flodden Field. Moreover, the King, being totally disinterested in Surrey's offer, on quitting Ford Castle had burnt it to the ground 'as it could not be defended' – so much for his chivalrous nature!

When William Heron died, in 1536, he left no son so that the estate passed from his family in the same way it had come to him, through the marriage of a daughter (though not without violent opposition from other members of the Heron family) to Thomas Carr of Etal.

The castle, having been extensively repaired in 1548 (after its wanton destruction in 1513) it was called upon the following year to again withstand a Scottish siege. The castles of Cornhill and Etal having already fallen the fury of the invader was then directed, mercilessly, at the fortification at Ford. The Scots' French allies, with their heavy field guns, wrought terrible damage to the castle's walls and towers but the garrison (under the valiant leadership of Thomas Carr) offered brave resistance "disputing every foot of ground". Carr is believed to have held out in the north-west tower, the castle's strongest point. Eventually, the Scots retired from the scene leaving Ford's jubilant defenders still in possession of their half-ruined stronghold.

The last time the castle was required to resist the advances of an enemy was in 1557, when Lord Hume, at the head of yet another Scottish army, threatened Ford. However, the approach of Sir Henry Percy deterred Hume and he retreated forthwith without inflicting any real damage on the castle. Thomas Carr left an heiress who married Sir Francis Blake. Blake, in turn, saw his heiress marry Edward Duval. The last to hold the Ford estate bearing this proud name was Edward's grandson. Yet, despite this peer being one of several brothers, remarkably, each of them died before they could inherit and so, once more, the castle and the estate exchanged hands. A daughter of the last Lord Delaval married Lord Tyrconnel and a grandson of this marital union became the Marquis of Waterford.

The Castle (Ford)

The Portcullis Gate is the entrance on the south front, in the centre of a semi-hexagonal projection, on each side of which is a wing, jutting out from a square turret and forming a spacious courtyard.

The entrance was formerly not on the south side, however, but on the west "where the village then lay close under the walls for safety" – a site now occupied by a formal garden.

The forecourt walls are castellated with higher corner towers.

Photographed by kind permission of Ford and Etal Estates (Lord Joicey).

The Castle (Ford)

The Portcullis Gate and the courtyard and castle entrance beyond.

Photographed by kind permission of Ford and Etal Estates (Lord Joicey).

The Castle (Ford)

The greatest part of the present building is the work of Sir John Hussey Delaval and was erected between 1761-4, in a style that has been described as "ginger-bread Gothic".

Sir John's immediate reaction on seeing the castle's condition at the time was that it was 'in ruins and uninhabitable'. Nevertheless, he repaired it at a cost of £10,500 so that the medieval fortress could become 'a useful and noble country seat'.

Much of Sir John's architecture was later altered or entirely removed by the Edinburgh architect, David Bryce, between the years 1861-5, when he was employed by Louisa, Marchioness of Waterford, and "which restored the castle (so it was claimed) to something of its ancient grandeur".

The Castle   (Ford)

The Cow or Flag Tower occupied the south-west corner of the courtyard. It stands alone, with its recessed upper stage and eighteenth century battlements.

Photographed by kind permission of Ford and Etal Estates (Lord Joicey).

The Castle (Ford)

In the 16th century Northumbrian noblemen were still unable to build fine mansions to match those of the landed gentry elsewhere because of the unsettled, even dangerous situation on the border with Scotland: protection and safety were still far more important than style and comfort!

No big new houses were built during this period and, at Ford alone, among the major buildings, were any domestic improvements made.

Here, before the end of the century, but still within the protection of its stout curtain walls, a new south front was added to the existing north range; in the common Elizabethan 'E-plan' – ie two storeys with attics and basement, with big, regular, mullioned and transomed windows. The front was remodelled, to some extent, in 1694, by Sir Francis Blake, who inserted new windows. Much later, during the course of work carried out by David Bryce (1861-5) for Louisa, Marchioness of Waterford, Bryce replaced the existing Gothic windows with 17th century style cross-windows.

The Castle (Ford)

The King James Tower.

In 1549 the Scots, together with their French allies, attacked the castle with its heavy field guns. They inflicted great damage on the walls and towers yet the castle's defenders held out bravely and eventually the Scots retired from the scene.

It is believed that the remnants of the garrison, under the leadership of Thomas Carr, made their final stand in the strongest part of the castle – the King James Tower.

Including the basement the tower is five storeys and has a mural stairway from the first to the second floor.

The Castle   (Ford)

The north front.

The castle consisted of a square courtyard with a rectangular tower at each corner. The two larger towers were to the north: the five storeyed King James Tower, in the north-west corner (right) and the north-east tower (left), which may have been an earlier hall-house and which was incorporated into the later castle.

These two towers were later joined together to make a mansion-house. David Bryce, the Edinburgh architect who carried out alterations to the castle between 1861-5 added terracing to the north side but all trace of it is gone now.

The Castle (Ford)

The gateway to the east (the 'Clock Tower') has two circular towers with friezes of little hanging intersected arches and quadrefoil openings below their battlements.

Photographed by kind permission of Ford and Etal Estates (Lord Joicey).

The Game Larder situated to the north-east of the castle, has been attributed to the Edinburgh architect, David Bryce, who carried out extensive alterations to Ford during the years 1861-5.

Round, with an overhanging conical roof and little square windows with moulded surrounds just below the eaves.

The Church of St Michael and All Angels (Ford)

St Michael's Church was standing here, overlooking the Cheviot Hills, before the nearby castle was even built. In 1853, Newcastle architect, John Dobson, added the north aisle, heightened the roof of the nave, redesigned the chancel and enlarged the chancel arch. He also added the south entrance porch. The windows throughout the church were redesigned and an old lancet in the west wall, which had previously been blocked up, was restored and is now fitted with a stained glass window, featuring St Michael. Dobson was accused of 'over-restoring the church' and that he had 'obliterated many of the church's most interesting features'.

Tomlinson, on the other hand, writes that "the work was executed with such good taste that the antique charm of the building has not been destroyed".

The Church of St Michael and All Angels (Ford)

During his extensive restoration work of 1853-4 John Dobson dramatically enlarged the chancel arch and redesigned the chancel itself.

The Church of St Michael and All Angels   (Ford)

The south entrance porch was added in 1853-4.

The magnificent bell-cote possibly belonged to the original building 'and is of a rare type built against the west wall like a big buttress and with a pyramidal cap and window, like openings for the bells'.

The Church of St Michael and All Angels (Ford)

The outside of the church has much to show of interest. All the windows, which were re-modelled by John Dobson in 1853-4, have simple hood-moulds each of which bears two stone, carved faces.

"It is difficult to say", writes the author of the church notes, "whether these were the work of nineteenth century stone-masons or whether they were old stones from some other building, re-used in this charming way".

Lady Waterford's Grave (Ford)

In the graveyard of the Church of St Michael and All Angels is the monument to Louisa, Marchioness of Waterford (at Ford Castle), who died in 1891.

Two kneeling angels hold a shield bearing the Waterford coat-of-arms. Lying horizontally on the stone-surrounded grave is a large, inscribed Celtic cross.

The Village   (Ford)

Lady Waterford began building her 'model' village of Ford, to the east of the castle c1860. The village consists of only one street.

The original houses, 'grey and joyless', are on the right side, those built by Lord Joicey c1914, are on the left.

At the very top of the street (east) stands the Jubilee Cottage of 1887.

The Village   (Ford)

The Lady Waterford Gallery, built in 1860 to be the village school and now a museum and the village hall, is a high Victorian Tudor building with mullioned windows, richly patterned roof and high steep gables bearing roundels with both the date and the Waterford coat-of-arms.

The information board, standing outside the entrance, reads as follows:

'The Lady Waterford Gallery. Formerly Ford School, with murals by Louisa, Marchioness of Waterford (1818-91).

The mural paintings around this building, which was the village school of Ford, until 1957, are the work of Louisa, Marchioness of Waterford. Widowed at the age of forty, she came to live at Ford Castle in 1859 and soon after decided to decorate her new school with her own paintings of scenes from the Bible.

Most of the characters were drawn from life from the villagers and school children of Ford, who went to sit for her in her studio in the castle. A prolific water colour artist from her early childhood, Louisa Waterford is now recognised as one of the most interesting women artists of the Victorian period.

The murals are her largest work. Some of her other works are also displayed in the Gallery, which is open throughout the year."

The Village   (Ford)

The Lady Joicey Memorial Hall is one of the most attractive buildings, built by Lord Joicey. The house, on the north side of the street, carries a date stone showing the year 1913.

Photographed by kind permission of Ford and Etal Estates (Lord Joicey).

The Village (Ford)

Situated at the west end of the one village street (nearest the castle) stands a polished, Aberdeen granite memorial to the Marquis of Waterford, dated 1859.

On the top of the pedestal there is an angel, facing west: on the base, inlaid, is the Waterford coat-of-arms.

Photographed by kind permission of Ford and Etal Estates (Lord Joicey).

On the base of the memorial to the Marquis of Waterford, inlaid, is the family coat-of-arms.

Photographed by kind permission of Ford and Etal Estates (Lord Joicey).

The Village   (Ford)

At the east end of the single street stands (facing west) stone-built, Jubilee Cottage (number 16), of 1887.

It has mullioned, twin-light windows either side of the centre gable: above the doorway is an 'embossed' picture of Queen Victoria and the date of her Golden Jubilee.

Photographed by kind permission of Ford and Etal Estates (Lord Joicey).

The Village   (Ford)

Only a few yards to the left of Jubilee Cottages stands the Blacksmith's Workshop.

Built in 1863 (there is a date-stone, surmounted by a crown, set into the north gable); single storey with a large stone horseshoe as a door surround and 'patterned on a smaller one in County Wexford (Ireland)'.

Heatherslaw Mill (near Etal)

The earliest parts of this fine Northumbrian water-mill may well date from the middle of the 18th century but most of the building is nineteenth century.

The mill was still in use until 1946.

Two bays and three storeys there is an attached three storey, five bays granary block, constructed c1805, which may have been used for malting.

The mill (and granary) are built of course rubble with well-dressed openings: they have hipped, blue-slated roofs.

Photographed by kind permission of Ford and Etal Estates (Lord Joicey).

Heatherslaw Mill   (near Etal)

The only water-mill in Northumberland open to the public.

The Light Railway (Heatherslaw)

"Clive", the stand-by diesel locomotive.

The Light Railway   (Heatherslaw)

The Railway Shed and 'Lady Augusta' ready for her trip to Etal.

The Railway opened in July, 1989 and everything needed has been manufactured on site, in the workshops, except the steam engine 'Lady Augusta'.

The engine was supplied new in 1989 and is an 0-4-2, solid fuel burning engine. It has been extensively modified since its arrival and now has ball and roller bearings, disc brakes and manganese steel tyres. The replacement of all the other wheels has considerably improved the running and performance of the locomotive. It is quite probably the only steam engine in the world fitted with disc brakes for additional safety.

The Light Railway   (Heatherslaw)

Leaving Heatherslaw on her short journey to Etal.

Normally there is an hourly service from Heatherslaw starting from the beginning of April, until the end of October, beginning at eleven o'clock; and an hourly service back again from Etal which begins at half past eleven.

The Village (Etal)

The tiny village of Etal stands beside the River Till, a tributary of the Tweed, and has been described as a more "natural" village than its neighbour – the "planned" village of Ford.

Etal has a ruined, mid – 14th century castle; a Georgian manor house; a splendid inn – Northumberland's only thatched inn, which was burnt down in 1980 but rebuilt exactly as before – and rows of what Nancy Mitford describes as "picture postcard" cottages.

The Village   (Etal)

The low, white – painted cottages may be less "trim and dainty" than those in nearby Ford but, it has been suggested, their attractiveness is due to their "peculiar air of antiquity". However by the end of the nineteenth century these same delightful cottages were in quite appalling condition. Indeed, in 1882, one local newspaper described them as "unfit for human habitation."

Some are quaintly thatched (like the Black Bull Inn), as so many were in this part of Northumberland, at the beginning of the twentieth century; others are roofed in big, rough, stone slates.

They owe their present, impeccable appearance to Lord Joicey, who rebuilt most of them c.1907.

Flodden Field   (Branxton)

The Battle of Flodden was fought between the English and the Scots on September 9th, 1513.

Although James IV of Scotland and Henry VIII of England had a 'treaty of perpetual friendship' and were, in fact, brothers-in-law, Scotland had a treaty with France which went back even further so that when Henry invaded France, in June 1513, James saw this as an opportunity to go to the assistance of an old ally and exploit the situation to both his and France's advantage. He believed that with the bulk of Henry's army in France England would be an easy prey with only a weekend force left behind to guard and defend the country.

James crossed the Tweed, near Coldstream, on August 22nd, with a force estimated at between 80,000 and 100,000 men. But, despite the huge army at his disposal – it was almost twice what the English could muster – James had seriously underestimated the resolve and capability of the force rallied and commanded, in Henry's absence, by Thomas Howard, the Earl of Surrey.

The story of the Battle of Flodden has been written about very many times. James IV, with his superior numbers, enjoyed a number of early successes: various border fortresses, including the castles at Norham and Ford, were easily destroyed yet, despite the numerical advantage the Scots enjoyed, James was unable to press home his advantage.

Not all his clan chiefs were reliable; there were too many desertions; many of his men were poorly armed and had virtually no military training to speak of. Crucially, the Scots had no answer to the skill of the English bowmen or the wielders of their frightening battle-axes. But most tellingly, perhaps, James threw away his biggest advantage – his position on the high ground – to accept battle on what was really Surrey's terms. Having first destroyed the Scottish 'wings' Surrey was then able to concentrate on the centre of the Scots' army where the King himself, surrounded by the 'flower' of his nobility, headed the conflict. To Scots everywhere the Battle of Flodden arouses only bitter memories. James was killed as were three bishops, thirteen earls and a host of lesser nobles. Indeed, not a single family of note in Scotland was spared personal loss in the bloody encounter: all lost a father, brother or son on that dreadful day.

The Flodden Monument (Branxton)

On the crest of the hill where James IV is said to have been killed is a tall, Celtic cross of grey Aberdeen granite standing on a cairn of rough granite blocks. Set up by the Berwickshire Naturalists' Club it was unveiled in 1910 by Sir George Douglas, the poet and essayist of Kelso.

It is simply inscribed:

'Flodden 1513. To the brave of both nations.'

The Church of St Paul (Branxton)

A church has existed in Branxton since the 12th century: its list of Vicars dates from 1200.

The present building was practically rebuilt in 1849 using a dark-brown igneous rock called rhyolite – with sandstone dressings. The church has been reconstructed, again, in the Norman style of architecture.

The site of the Battle of Flodden (1513) is only a short distance south of St Paul's. It is said that the dead and dying of both nations, English and Scots, were given shelter, care and attention to both their physical and spiritual needs, within the walls of the ancient Norman structure – only one fragment of which remains: the chancel arch, which is from the Transitional period.

The north-west tower has a pyramidal roof.

The Collingwood Arms (Cornhill on Tweed)

The coloured inn sign, above and to the left of the entrance porch, is a picture of John Collingwood, always referred to locally as 'the Squire'. The inn still retains its offer of 'Post Horses' in large lettering. Inside the hotel is a photograph of the building dated 1865: from its appearance it looked like an old building even then. It possibly dates from the 18th century though no records seem to exist.

Pevsner refers to it simply as 'an early 19th century coaching inn, with seven bays'.

Cornhill House (Cornhill on Tweed)

W W Tomlinson writes: "Nothing remains of the ancient tower of 'Cornell', which was destroyed by the Earl of Fife in 1385, rebuilt by the Swinhoes and taken by the French General D'Esse, at the head of a group of Scots in 1549. It was standing in 1560."

Brian Long also states that the Earl destroyed the tower in 1385 'but it was rebuilt and described as new in 1541'. 'The owner at that time', Long continues, 'was also building a barmkin around the same'.

Eric Grounds, the present owner of Cornhill House confirms much of this when he says that in 1549 the house was attacked by Scots whose French commander D'Esse, reported that the house was 'surrounded by a stout barmkin and well supplied with fish!'

Mr Grounds informs me that there was some form of fortified Keep on the site of Cornhill House before it was burnt to the ground in 1385 then rebuilt by the de Swinhoes. Gilbert de Swinhoe married a de Grey, the original owners of the Cornhill property. The marriage only produced daughters, however, one of whom married a Forster. The Forsters enlarged the house substantially. Eventually, the Forsters, too, 'ran into daughters', one of whom married a Collingwood of Eslington – of which family a great number populated Northumberland at that time.

Henry Collingwood, of Lilburn and Cornhill, sold Lilburn to a cousin (another Collingwood) and moved his family to Cornhill. Henry and his son, Henry John William Collingwood were High Sheriffs of Northumberland, in 1793 and 1832 respectively.

The great grandson of H J W Collingwood was John Henry Francis Collingwood who married a lady from New Zealand by the name of Nancy Moss. They had no children; moreover, Nancy refused to live at Cornhill and eventually 'their marriage fell apart'. John then had 'an enduring love affair' with one Nancy Hudleston, a second cousin of Nancy Moss and the aunt of the present owner, Eric Grounds.

The Cornhill estate was sold over a two year period, 1976-78, some two years after the death of John Collingwood. Sadly the estate was sold 'piecemeal' … one farm to one buyer; a second farm to another: woodland to another and the river to yet two further families. Fortuitously, the house was bought by a lady called Marie Packshaw who, after only seven years in residence, decided she wanted to 'move on'.

Cornhill House (Cornhill on Tweed)

Described as 'a picturesque building in the Elizabethan style' and by E Mackenzie, in 1825, as 'the ancient, cross-shaped seat of the Collingwoods' the house is, indeed, a cruciform shape – white painted, irregular and 'very Scottish in feel', with steeply pitched roofs and crow stepped gables. The base of the western gable-end probably dates from the mid-14th century: there is a large, semi-circular arch in the sitting room (part of the original building) which seems to be of the period.

Photographed by kind permission of Mr Eric Grounds.

Cornhill House   (Cornhill on Tweed)

During the tenure of the Forsters the original bastle, or pele tower, became a long, barn-like structure, facing south. Over the years additional wings were added.

The walls of that part of the house which runs from east to west are more than three feet thick.

Photographed by kind permission of Mr Eric Grounds.

Cornhill House   (Cornhill on Tweed)

Through his various connections (the owner was a member of the Queen's Dragoon Guards), when Marie Packshaw decided to sell the property he was able to purchase the house (in the mid-80s) where he had spent his childhood raised by his aunt, Nancy Hudleston.

Mr Grounds believes his to be the only house in England facing south across the Tweed, towards the distant hills and into Scotland.

The weather vane on the outbuilding certainly seems to endorse the owner's claim.

Cornhill House   (Cornhill on Tweed)

The weather vane on the adjacent outbuilding shows quite clearly that the house does, indeed, face south into Scotland.

Cornhill House (Cornhill on Tweed)

The red-brick stable-block was built in 1897.

The Collingwood coat-of-arms inside the almost Venetian-style window above the entrance archway shows a stag standing beneath a tree.

In olden times a stag was nicknamed a 'Colin': the tree obviously symbolises a 'wood' – thus, 'Collingwood'.

Cornhill House (Cornhill on Tweed)

The stable-block of 1897 stands south of the house and, as the weather-vane shows, faces south looking over the River Tweed into Scotland.